ONE PILGRIM'S
PROGRESS

How to Build a World-Class Company, and Who to Credit

BO PILGRIM

NELSON BUSINESS
A Division of Thomas Nelson Publishers
Since 1798

www.thomasnelson.com

Published in Nashville, Tennessee, by Thomas Nelson, Inc.

Nelson Books titles may be purchased in bulk for educational, business, fundraising, or sales
promotional use. For information, please email SpecialMarkets@ThomasNelson.com.

ISBN: 0-7852-1190-X (HC)
ISBN: 0-7852-1875-0 (SE, HC)
ISBN: 0-7852-1876-9 (SE, TP)

Printed in the United States of America
05 06 07 08 09 BTY 9 8 7 6 5 4 3 2 1

To Patty, my loving wife of 49 years . . . to our three children,
Ken, Greta, and Pat . . . and to our six grandchildren—for
their love, dedication, and support that I can always
count on—and to our memories past, present,
and those yet to be. I love you. —Daddy Bo

Contents

FOREWORD

OFFICE OF THE GOVERNOR

RICK PERRY
GOVERNOR

When I think of entrepreneurial icons—men and women who are dreamers and doers—I think of legends like Bo Pilgrim.

A man of faith, an entrepreneur with a vision, and a leader who gives back to his community, Bo Pilgrim started Pilgrim's Pride in the rural East Texas town of Pittsburg, where the company's world headquarters remains today as a reminder of his pledge to revitalize rural America for this generation and the ones to come.

As Governor of the State of Texas, and a personal friend to Bo and the Pilgrim family, I hope you will enjoy reading *One Pilgrim's Progress*—the story of a driven individual's entrepreneurial voyage to the top starting from the ground up.

Bo is a unique American figure. And his life is a window into the recipe for success: hard work, belief, perseverance and vision. *One Pilgrim's Progress* is a compelling story for all looking to learn what it takes to grow, succeed and prosper.

Rick Perry
Governor of Texas

Rick Perry

PREFACE

The faith, drive, and determination of Bo Pilgrim have taken a small feed store and turned it into a Fortune 500 company with more than 40,000 employees in 71 cities and 17 states in the United States of America, and operations in Mexico and Puerto Rico. Pilgrim's Pride Corporation is listed on the New York Stock Exchange under the symbol PPC. It ships products to 70 nations outside the United States.

This book is about chickens, turkeys, and eggs, but especially about chickens. Pilgrim's Pride corporation is the second largest poultry operation in the world. It's a book about the free enterprise system in America that creates an environment for any person who seeks to be among the 1 percent of all human beings who excel in any business of his or her own choice. It's a story about optimism that something bigger and better can and does lie just around the next corner for those who are God-fearing, hard-working, right-living, freedom-loving people.

Can you imagine producing 6 million chickens for market each day?

Most people can't. But Bo Pilgrim never doubted that God wanted him to dream about such big numbers.

Years ago Bo was asked in jest the proverbial question about whether the chicken or the egg came first. Bo didn't hesitate. "The chicken," he said. When asked how he could be so sure, Bo opened a Bible on a table nearby. He read aloud these words about the fifth day of creation in the first chapter of the Bible: "God created . . . every winged bird according to its kind. And God saw that it was good. And God blessed them, saying, 'Be fruitful and multiply . . . and let birds multiply on the earth'" (Gen. 1:21–22 NKJV). Bo said with his enigmatic smile as he closed the book: "Chickens and turkeys are winged birds!"

And then he added, "Six million a day . . . is a good number for God to multiply."

INTRODUCTION:
IT'S A MIND-BOGGLING THING

The world's experts will tell you that you can't mix business with spiritual matters. I'm here to say otherwise. Spiritual things can coexist with good business principles. I've been proving that statement true for more than sixty years.

My name is Bo Pilgrim, and I am the cofounder, largest stockholder, and chairman of the board of Pilgrim's Pride Corporation, the second largest poultry producer in the United States and Mexico, and the largest producer of chicken in Puerto Rico. The facts and figures related to Pilgrim's Pride are mind-boggling:

- We do $5.4 billion worth of business a year.
- We have more than 40,000 employees who we call our "Partners."
- Every day our plants produce chicken for 46.8 million people and eggs for 2 million people.
- We have 71 locations in 17 U.S. states.
- We produce almost 6 billion pounds of dressed chicken and turkey a year, including further-processed prepared foods, with branded items for retail, quick-service restaurants, and foodservice marketing.
- We also produce table eggs, hatching eggs, and chicken feed. Our commercial feed division manufactures high-quality bulk and bagged feed for livestock and show animals.

- We operate hatcheries, feed mills, chicken-processing plants, further-processing plants for chicken, cooking facilities, turkey-processing plants and further-processing plants for turkey, distribution centers, protein conversion and wastewater treatment plants.
- We contract with 5,000 contract growers in the United States and Mexico.
- We process, package, and distribute more than 1,000 different products every day. In just one of our processing plants—located in Mount Pleasant, Texas—we have the capability of producing 2,000 different products and the capacity to turn out more than 7 million pounds of finished goods per week.
- A distribution center near Pittsburg, Texas, features a state-of-the-art, fully automated, 40-million-pound-capacity freezer featuring Radio Frequency Identification (RFID) and Global Positioning System (GPS) technologies, allowing worldwide inventory tracking.
- We export products to more than 70 nations, including China, Japan, Kazakhstan, and Russia.

These are mind-boggling facts!

Even more mind-boggling to many people is that I don't take credit for these accomplishments of the company that bears my name. I know Who to credit for this international success story in business: the Lord Jesus Christ. I've taken His principles and put them into practice in the world of business—nothing more, but nothing less.

I've been praised for having a down-to-earth style. My greatest claim to fame, however, is that I know the One who God, our Creator and heavenly Father, sent down to this earth to change the hearts of men and women and to free them from sin's bondage.

I've been applauded for innovation and marketing ability to produce one of the most recognizable brands in the food industry. In truth, God the Creator is the One who gives all good ideas—we simply carry them out in practical ways as the Lord leads us, in any field in which we work.

I've been introduced as a man who exhibits honesty and respect for others. I know, however, that it is the Holy Spirit who produces in a person the character qualities that are the most effective in influencing people and pointing others toward Christ.

I've been called a leader. In truth, I know the One to follow.

I've gained a reputation as a man who has helped thousands of people make a good living. In reality, I'm far more concerned with helping people learn how to *live*—how to love and serve God with their whole hearts, minds, and strength.

If you are looking only for a business book with good management principles, this book isn't for you. If you need management training, I recommend the excellent books and courses published by the American Management Association.

If you are looking for a book that will tell you secret shortcuts to overnight success, this book isn't for you. It's taken me seventy-seven years to get to this point, both in business and in life, and God isn't through with me yet. I don't believe in shortcuts. I don't believe overnight success is likely or likely to be sustained.

But . . . if you are looking for a story about how God can use one person to make a difference, this book is for you. What God has done in my life, He not only *can* do, but *wants* to do in your life. Let Him have His way and His say . . . and He'll lead you to the greatest heights you can ever know, not only in business, but in all areas of your life.

The truly mind-boggling fact is that God can take an ordinary human life from an ordinary place and do extraordinary things.

I

I WAS ALWAYS
GOING SOMEWHERE

The deal was the largest in the history of the poultry industry—valued at more than $600 million. It was certainly the largest deal I had ever had anything to do with.

The deal made Pilgrim's Pride Corporation the second largest poultry producer in the world—almost twice the size of the third-place poultry producer in the U.S. The deal put us into new markets internationally and gave us new potential for growth and development.

The deal to which I am referring is the acquisition of the ConAgra chicken division by Pilgrim's Pride Corporation in autumn 2003.

The deal took many people by surprise, but in truth, the relationships that underscored its success had been growing for some time.

Through the years, I had met the leaders of ConAgra's chicken division at various industry meetings. We had developed a friendship, even though we were competitors, and we admired each other's business principles. At several of these industry meetings, I had opportunities to converse with poultry company executives about our strategy of seeking to add more value to all of our products and services. Bruce Rohde, who was then president and chief executive officer of ConAgra Foods, and Dwight Goslee, who was then executive president for operations, control, and development of ConAgra Foods, seemed to be on the same page with me when it came to the way we approached customer service and business growth and development.

Finding ways to add more value to products and services has been a focus of Pilgrim's Pride for decades. Through the years, we had grown internally, but we also had taken advantage of several strategic acquisition opportunities that enabled us to expand our product mix and our distribution capabilities—especially when it came to prepared foods. I knew enough from these previous acquisitions to be able to envision numerous ways in which Pilgrim's Pride and ConAgra's chicken division might enhance each other.

The discussions about how Pilgrim's Pride and ConAgra's chicken division might work together began in earnest in early May 2003. I initiated several telephone conversations with Dwight Goslee, and I specifically asked to meet with him and Bruce Rohde face-to-face to discuss a larger acquisition of ConAgra's chicken operations than various lower-level executives at ConAgra had been willing to discuss with us. Rohde and Goslee agreed to the meeting, and on May 9, 2003, I traveled with Cliff Butler, our vice chairman, and Rick Cogdill, our executive vice president and chief financial officer, to meet with Rohde and Goslee in Omaha, Nebraska.

At that meeting we laid out our plan for and interest in acquiring *all* of ConAgra's chicken operations for approximately $600 million in assets for $100 million in cash, common stock representing approximately 40 to 45 percent of the total consideration, and a subordinated note for the balance, which we asked ConAgra to carry for us. After a few hours of working through various details, we had forged the general framework of an agreement. We discussed the next moves—the required documentation and meetings with our respective boards—and we agreed to move forward to see whether the transaction could be completed.

For the next four weeks, both corporations experienced a flurry of activity. We dispatched our operations people to visit all of the major ConAgra chicken division facilities. We had the legal, tax, and accounting professionals conducting legal and financial due diligence on ConAgra's chicken business and financial records. We had investment bankers working to render fairness opinions. Banks were lined up to provide the key elements of the financing. Cogdill for Pilgrim's Pride and Goslee for ConAgra hammered out the structure of the legal agreement.

Then, on Saturday, June 7, 2003, we had a special meeting of our board of directors to consider and give final approval to the proposed transaction. The proposal before our board passed unanimously.

The final $600-plus million for which Pilgrim's Pride Corporation obligated itself now carries a public value realized to ConAgra in return for its chicken division of more than $1 billion in total value, when valuing the stock portion of the consideration at current trading levels. It was, and continues to be, a win-win deal for both companies.

In the deal, Pilgrim's Pride Corporation doubled its operations in most areas. We jumped to $5.6 billion a year in annualized sales, more than 40,000 Partners (employees), and a market share of more than 15 percent. We added 44.1 million pounds to our ready-to-cook production of chicken—up to 109.1 million pounds of ready-to-cook chicken on an average weekly basis. The producer just behind us produces only 61.8 million pounds of ready-to-cook chicken on an average weekly basis. We have almost twice the people, twice the markets, twice the revenue, twice the distribution of this next-largest competitor. That's a stretch.

Was I excited about this deal?

I don't know that I'd use the word *excited*. *Challenged*, perhaps. Ready to take on the challenge? Absolutely. In many ways, it felt like the next logical step to take, albeit a large step.

Was I surprised at how quickly and easily the deal fell into place? No, I wasn't. When things are right—a win-win for both parties—deals often fall into place quickly.

Was I pleased that the deal came about so smoothly? Definitely. Rohde made it clear that the deal came down to a single factor that I've come to recognize and value increasingly through the years: integrity.

Although integrity might not be considered a financial factor, it's certainly at the root of all good financial decisions and business choices. Rohde and I had a relationship. We trusted each other. He saw me as a man of good business principles and integrity. I saw him the same way. We could forge a $600-plus million deal in a matter of a few hours because integrity was our foundation.

A $600 million deal would have been beyond my wildest imagination seventy years ago. What would a boy from Pine, Texas—population less than one hundred people—know about business deals of that magnitude? In a word . . . nothing.

But what would a boy from Pine, Texas, know about integrity—about being true to your word, standing on principle, and developing relationships that transcend the decades?

Everything.

> *Although integrity might not be considered a financial factor, it's certainly at the root of all good financial decisions and business choices . . . We could forge a $600-plus million deal in a matter of a few hours because integrity was our foundation.*

Pine might have been small, but the principles I learned there were lasting and huge. The relationships I developed there continue today. The way I did business there—even as a boy selling soda pop—is very much the way I do business today: honest, straightforward, and at a fair profit.

To understand the success of Pilgrim's Pride Corporation . . . to understand my personal success . . . you need to understand my roots.

A Boy from Pine with Deep Roots

My name really is Bo. I was born May 8, 1928, and was officially named Lonnie Pilgrim in honor of my father, whose name was Alonzo, but from my earliest days, relatives called me Bo. It's the name I've always used.

I was the fourth of seven children—two more children died as infants. My brother Harold was ten years older than I. Brother Aubrey and sister Mary Katheryn were also older. Billy, Sue, and Margaret were younger siblings.

We lived in Pine, Texas, a community of eighty-to-one-hundred people during my growing-up years.

We were poor—but so was everybody else. In fact, the whole nation was poor in the early 1930s, but one of the poorer places in America was East Texas. People were trying to scratch out a living by growing cotton and potatoes, and raising cattle, but neither was very profitable in those days. Most people who raised cattle also grew a little corn to feed them, and in a smaller garden, they grew crops for their own table.

For a small town, Pine actually had a significant amount of industry. It had a sawmill, a shingle mill, a cotton gin, a potato house, a school, two stores, a post office, and a railroad going right through the center of the town. The community was organized in 1884 and was called Pine Tree because of all the pines in the area. Earlier, the small town was called Cannon Switch in honor of the Reverend Burell Cannon, who built what he called the *Ezekiel Airship* after the description of a flying machine in the biblical book of Ezekiel. Later, the town was called Cannon Ball because of the train station and tracks through town. In 1884, however, the name was Pine Tree, and a few years later, the *Tree* was dropped.

My father operated one of the two stores in Pine. The other store was founded by Dr. W. T. Efurd, who had a certificate of medicine but decided not to practice after he opened the store in 1892. Efurd was a teacher, store-keeper, and preacher. The Pine Grocery and Post Office, which was my father's store, was across the street from Efurd's Store. Our store offered all kinds of canned vegetables and fruits, as well as canned fish. My father also carried an assortment of dry goods, from tobacco to flour. That certainly wasn't the only enterprise my father had, however—after all, he had seven children to feed in addition to himself and my mother, Gertrude.

The train that ran through Pine began to stop in Pine after Efurd's Store opened. A person could take the train six miles away to Pittsburg, Texas, for fifteen cents—or hang onto the side of a freight train for nothing. Unfortunately the train stopped only once a day at nine o'clock in the morning, and it didn't run back through Pine, so whoever took the train to Pittsburg needed to find another way home. I learned that the hard way one day when, as a boy, I sneaked onto the train and found myself with a real adventure trying to get home before I was missed.

We had a switch track in Pine that ran parallel to the main track, and also a third track. It was on this third track we loaded logs onto railcars. The logs were about four feet long and two feet in diameter. They had been cut to be shipped. Two long "skinned" pine limbs were leaned into a boxcar door from the ground, and then logs were brought into the yard for transport. My father would buy those logs and roll them up the skids into the cars. He didn't do the work by himself, of course. Hired men helped. I was always amazed at their strength and skill in handling the logs—they could take a log and flip it over on their knees to stack the logs two high in the boxcar.

My father also bought cotton in Pine, and I remember playing on those bales of cotton between the store and the house. Cotton became so cheap at one point that Daddy burned cotton bales because they had no value. I also remember that beef at one time was so cheap that people couldn't afford to raise cattle—the cost of the feed was more than what they could get for the animal once it was grown.

In addition to the grocery, our family had a large potato house where people would bring their potatoes to be washed, graded, and stored until they were shipped out by train. When I was only ten years old, I hung potato bags in a shop next door to the store. My father bought potatoes in bulk, and I put them into the bags for resale. I made a dollar a week doing that, and I spent that money going to Pittsburg to the picture show where I enjoyed the movies while eating a bag of popcorn.

The church and the school initially were located in the same building, but by the time I was born, the town had a church and a school in separate buildings. The school building had two main classrooms separated by a center hall, and a larger room that served as an auditorium. Two teachers and a principal instructed about forty children total in all eight grades.

Today, the Pine Baptist Church, the Pine Grocery, the Pine Community Center, and scattered chicken houses are all that remain in Pine.

Lessons in Working and Selling

Pine might not have had much to offer in the way of luxury or prosperity, but it did have lots of opportunities for work. I learned how to work as a boy, and I learned how to sell.

We lived two or three hundred yards behind the store, and as I grew up, one of the things I considered a major treat was a Coca-Cola. I frequently went to the store to ask my father for a Coke. When I was only about six years old, my father taught me what it meant to be an entrepreneur. I asked Daddy for a Coca-Cola one day, and he said, "Okay, Bo, you can have a Coke, but what I want you to do first is to take six Cokes down to the gin"—which Calvin Gunn, my grandfather, owned—"and sell those Cokes and bring me back the money and I'll give you a Coke." I sold six Cokes, each for five cents, and for that I got one Coke free. I was selling on commission!

Hauling a six-pack of Cokes to the gin was a major effort for me as a boy, so I had a second learning opportunity—to invent something that might make my work easier. I built a little wagon from a set of hand-me-down wheels. I took two two-by-fours and cut them the length of the wheel axles front and back, attached the wheels, and then connected them with two-by-fours. This gave the wagon a turning radius on the front end, guided by a grass rope that I held in my hand. On top of the "wagon" I put a potato crate, and I set my Cokes in that crate. I'm not sure where I learned how to make that little wagon—it just seemed something obvious to me as a means of making my work easier. It did the job.

I found that selling the Cokes was easy, but collecting the money for the drinks was sometimes difficult. Sometimes a man would say, "I just paid you, Bo. It's that guy over there that hasn't paid you." I learned to keep careful track of who had paid and when, and I finally learned to hand a man a Coke only if he was handing five cents back to me.

I always felt a certain amount of pride and satisfaction after I had collected all the money and was pulling my empty wagon back down the ruts of the sandy road to the store to collect the reward of my entrepreneurship. Those Cokes I earned had a special taste all their own.

That was my first experience at earning money. I carried it proudly in my pocket, just as everybody else did who had any money. Nobody had surplus money in the mid-1930s. People had only the money in their pockets. And nobody knew for sure when the next bit of money might be coming.

The atmosphere was one of survival. I still have that feeling today in the pit of my stomach. It's a feeling that led me to work hard—to probably being a workaholic. It's a feeling that doesn't disappear, no matter how much money might be in the bank or in my wallet.

LESSONS IN A ROUGH-AND-TUMBLE ATMOSPHERE OF SURVIVAL

The lessons of survival were underscored by the simple fact that we lived in East Texas, and East Texas occasionally had violent storms.

In 1936 a storm blew into Pine from the west. It took the roof off our store and post office—the roof landed toward our home east of the store. The storm also hit our garage and picked it up from around our old

T-model car—the garage was blown away, but the car remained where it was sitting. We had neighbors to the south, about 150 yards away, and their house was blown away. Beyond that, as the storm moved to the east, it blew the potato house away. The potato house had a concrete foundation, and after the storm we used that flat, vacant foundation for many years as a place for country dances on Friday and Saturday nights. Young people from about a five-mile radius came to those dances.

LESSONS OF ANIMAL CARE

I also learned to care for animals as a boy. We had a Jersey cow by the name of Heart. Heart grazed by the side of the railroad that ran west of the store. The railroad that came through Pine was called the Cotton Belt. It ran from St. Louis, Missouri, to Tyler, Texas. Wild clover grew along the railroad tracks, and Heart always grazed there. It was my job in the late afternoon to make sure that Heart had been driven back to our own backyard so that when Daddy locked the store and post office in the late afternoon and came to the house, he could milk her. The milk from that cow was really our main source of protein.

No, we didn't raise chickens. That came later.

LESSONS IN FRIENDSHIP

I had several friends as a boy—some a year or two older, some a year or two younger. We were in school together, went to church together, played together, and pulled pranks together. We were boys, and that's the best excuse I can offer for some of the things we did.

I clearly remember times when J. S. Hackler came to Pine selling Coca-Cola off his truck to my father. We boys hung around outside and hid in a ditch near the store. As J. S. backed out and headed south down the little dirt road, we ran alongside the truck and pulled the exposed Cokes out of their cases and threw them in the soft dirt of the ditch to the side of the road. I don't know if J. S. allowed us to do that or not, but we thought we were doing "something big" to get those Cokes off that truck. I'm not sure we ever even thought of ourselves as stealing—acquiring Cokes from J. S. Hackler's truck was a game for us, and we all were eager to win.

LESSONS IN FAITH AND LIFE

It isn't that I grew up without a sense of right and wrong. At the time I was born, the Pine Baptist Church had about thirty members; just over half of those members were residents of Pine, and the rest came from nearby farms and even smaller communities. The church budget for the year 1930 was a whopping $218. We Pilgrim children attended regularly. I grew up knowing the Ten Commandments and Bible stories.

Daddy was also quick to tell me the right way to live. I'll never forget the day Daddy questioned me about whether I had been smoking. My friends and I had stolen some Bull Durham tobacco and hidden it in the depot, a little ways south from the store. Several of us boys—eight or nine years old at the time—went to the depot to smoke whenever we could sneak away from our families and our chores. We went to the depot because it wasn't active at the time. Daddy smelled smoke on my clothes after I had driven Heart back to the house one evening, and he gave me a real lecture about smoking that I never forgot. I quit smoking, and I never smoked after that except for a few cigars when I was in the service during the Korean War.

A BOY ON THE GO

While I remember some of these basic life lessons from my early days in Pine, I remember most clearly and with the greatest pleasure the days when I played with my childhood friends Rayford Taylor, Bruce Taylor, and James Shaddix in the sand underneath the front of our house. In Pine, you played in either sand or mud.

People didn't build level foundations for their houses the way they do now. Our house was on a slight hill with the back of the house on the higher side of the hill and posts holding up the front part of the house at the lower side of the hill. This type of construction resulted in a space left underneath the front part of the house. That was my playground.

My friends and I played what we called "cars"—except that I didn't have a car. I had only a hand-me-down steel skate. I took off the buckle and turned the skate around so the heel of the skate looked like the front of a truck to me, and the flat part of the skate became the bed of the truck. I burrowed out a system of roads in the sand under the house. My truck covered miles of dirt roads in any given week—the roads, of course, were intertwined in a fairly elaborate pattern under that old wood frame house.

All of it was in my imagination, but even as a young boy, I was going somewhere. It was always a joy for me to play with my system of roads and my truck . . . running my truck along the roads to different places that were also in my imagination. I have never forgotten that space or time. I remember those days with great pleasure.

> My friends and I played what we called "cars"—except that I didn't have a car. I had only a hand-me-down steel skate. I took off the buckle and turned the skate around so the heel of the skate looked like the front of a truck to me, and the flat part of the skate became the bed of the truck.

That didn't mean, however, that I ever imagined living anywhere but Pine. I wasn't dreaming of going somewhere far from home. I was dreaming of going somewhere in *life*. I was a boy always on the go, always on the move. And if a person could get somewhere faster by running, I ran. My friends recall that after school, we often made our way to my father's grocery store . . . running. Somehow I always managed to get there first. If a person could get there faster by driving a vehicle—even if that person could barely see over the dash and was far too young for a driver's license—well, so be it. I drove!

I had built-in energy then that I still have today.

I marvel at times that the imaginary truck on my imaginary roads has turned into a fleet of vehicles owned by Pilgrim's Pride. We have almost 5,000 total vehicles—including 18-wheeler trucks—on the road every day to move feed to the farms where our baby chicks are growing, move fully grown chickens to the processing plants, and move our processed chicken to wholesale outlets. These trucks traveled 77 million miles last year! They posted a very impressive safe driving rate of 0.65 recordable accidents per million miles. (The Department of Transportation's unsatisfactory recordable rate is 1.5.) The transportation division also has heavy trucks, cars and pickups, trailers, and off-road equipment. They are all going *somewhere* every day.

And so am I.

THREE DAYS THAT CHANGED
MY YOUNG LIFE FOREVER

Three days of my boyhood changed my life forever. The first of those days was the day my beloved father died of a heart attack—April 11, 1939. I was ten years old. Things were never the same for me. My mother took over the store and ran it for another twenty years—she also became the postmaster. Then she sold the store to my eldest brother, Harold.

A few Sundays after my father died, I made a personal commitment of my life to Jesus Christ. I knew that I needed to do that if I was going to be with my father in heaven someday. My love for my father was a strong motivation in my accepting the love of my heavenly Father. I have never regretted that decision, and I have never turned back on it. It was the second day that changed my life forever.

The third day that changed my life occurred when I was thirteen years old. My mother remarried after my father's death, and I didn't think she should have. My opinion was influenced greatly by the very strong opinions of my paternal grandmother, Ada Pilgrim, and my aunt Eva. Their opinions supported my intense feelings of loyalty and love for my father. In many ways, I felt my mother was betraying the excellence of my father and replacing him in her heart. That was unthinkable to me at the age of thirteen.

I took a very dramatic step of leaving my mother's home and moving to the house shared by my grandmother and aunt. I left home with a few meager personal belongings, nine hogs that I was raising as a Lone Star Farmers project at the time, and a hundred-pound bag of hog feed.

My grandfather had died some time before I made this move, so for several years, it was just Grandmother, Aunt Eva, and me working on my grandmother's farm. I lived there during my high school days.

We had no running water, no electricity, and no money on my grandmother's farm. We grew the food we ate. My grandmother also had land that was let out to sharecroppers, who paid in the form of food. We canned peas and corn, and raised chickens in the backyard. That was my first experience in raising chickens.

These chickens would run out in the yard, and since we didn't have a mower, we used a hoe to dig up the grass so the chickens could scratch in the sand. We covered their droppings so we didn't track them into the house. The old hens would lay eggs in the grass and sit on them and hatch out the baby chicks. Then we'd move the hen and baby chicks into a small house that looked a little like a doghouse. The chicks would follow their hen into the house at night, and we'd take a board and put it in front of

I left home with a few meager personal belongings, nine hogs that I was raising as a Lone Star Farmers project at the time, and a hundred-pound bag of hog feed.

the doorway of the house so the snakes, armadillos, possums, raccoons, and any other animals that might be roaming the neighborhood couldn't get to them.

We grew the chicks by feeding them corn we grew on the farm. We had to shell this corn, of course. The sheller was attached to a box, and after an ear was shucked, it was put into the sheller and pressed through the grinder. We fed some of the corn to the chicks and sold the rest to a peddler when he came to town. We traded extra chickens for coffee and tea and other things we weren't able to produce on the farm.

In addition to chickens, we ate pork. When the weather turned cold enough to keep meat cool, we would kill a hog and dress it out. We'd hang at least part of the meat from the rafters of the smokehouse. The meat was rubbed down by hand using different types of seasoning and curing agents. That was our source of meat that didn't decay for several months.

I learned how to cut mold off salt-cured pork that had been hanging in the shed . . . to use a common dipper in the water bucket . . . to fuel a cookstove with wood . . . and to wash in a basin on the porch. I worked at Alton Hill's grocery store after school and on Saturdays. I also bucked fifty-pound sacks of flour and hundred-pound sacks of wheat gray shorts, a byproduct of wheat fed to hogs. I might have been young, but I was strong! For a while, I also worked some nights shoveling dirt into three-yard dump trucks.

The first day I left home to live with my grandmother, I walked out in the front yard to a little knoll that had no grass on it. I sat down in the dirt there. It was getting late in the day, and as I looked to the west, the sun was starting to go down. It felt like a moment of a new beginning for me—certainly it was a moment of great change. I began to pray, and as I talked to Jesus, I told Him that if I ever amounted to anything, I would always give Him credit.

I'm still obligated to that. I have spent my youth and adult life doing my best to give Him the credit for anything I have accomplished. I'm now seventy-seven years old, and that commitment to the Lord is still a part of my desire—not to be a celebrity for myself but to be a celebrity for Him. It was a decision that changed my life and continues to shape my life.

Things to Count On and
Keep as Precious

I learned from my earliest memories that there are only a few things that a person can truly count on in this life—the presence of God and faith, the ties of family, the camaraderie of friends, the importance of hard work, and the need to be responsible for oneself and to use one's intelligence, skills, and abilities to reach one's God-given dreams. I also learned that the main reason to live is to bring glory to God the Creator, the One who gives us everything we have and who makes us into everything we'll ever be.

I can't think of any more important lessons for a boy to learn—or for any person to learn at any age. I've never regretted being a boy from Pine, Texas. That boyhood gave me all I needed as the basics for life.

★ ★ ★

That good thing which was committed to you, keep.
(2 Tim. 1:14 NKJV)

2

MOTIVATED BY SURVIVAL AND
CAPTIVATED BY OPPORTUNITY

One of the main cash crops in Camp County in the early 1930s was moonshine. Even though I was underage, I drove a truck delivering sugar and rye to the creek bottom for my brother Harold who was working with my mother in the store after my father died. I rolled the sacks of sugar and rye off the truck onto my knees and then lifted them the best I could and carried them to the side of the road and left them there. By the time I drove the truck to the top of the hill to turn around and returned to where I had rolled off the supplies . . . they were gone. I never saw who picked them up. We knew the supplies were for moonshine, but we never saw the moonshiners, and we never knew where the moonshine was sold.

Movies and television programs have somewhat glamorized the moonshine business, but let me assure you, it had to have been hard work. Most of the moonshining operations were in the deep woods, far from a person's home. The stills were connected to ten-gallon kegs that might produce five gallons of liquor. This generally had to be hauled out of the woods on a man's shoulders. Getting the moonshine to some form of market meant trying to outsmart the tax men (or revenuers), who were always on the lookout for the moonshiners who were breaking the law by avoiding paying taxes on their sales. Very often, stills had to be torn down and moved every few months in order to stay one step ahead of the law. It was a poor way to make a living. I'm grateful I never had to do that kind of work. But I also know what it means to be motivated by the need for *survival*. That was the motivation for just about everything my brother Aubrey and I did in our late teens and early twenties.

Aubrey was the one who got me into the chicken business. Actually he got me into a feed store business that *became* the chicken business.

Aubrey joined with a man named Pat Johns to purchase a feed and seed store from Pat's uncle, W. W. Weems, in Pittsburg, Texas. The price was $3,500. They put $1,000 down and signed a note with payments of $100 a month at 6 percent interest. A simple two-page typed document sealed the deal between my brother and Pat. It was the simplest of contracts with the simplest of terms. The deal was dated October 2, 1946. They called their store Farmer's Feed and Seed Co.—it was located at 115 Compress Street, not far from the intersection of two railroads in downtown Pittsburg.

Aubrey and Pat were not rich men—far from it. At the time they purchased the feed store from Weems, a rumor was floating around that each man thought the other had far more than the $500 he was putting into the venture. In truth, $500 was just about the total net worth of each man! The feed store was a big risk for both of them.

When they took over ownership of the feed store, U.S. farm prices were at their highest level since 1920. Chicken was in short supply, and in general, Americans were facing a severe meat crisis. Some people had even started eating horse meat. In Camp County where Pittsburg is located, agricultural income in 1946 came mostly from row crop farming, such as sweet potatoes, Irish potatoes, cotton, corn, and sorghum. There were more mules and wagons than tractors in our part of the nation.

My brother Aubrey knew very little about feed and seed. He had been hauling gravel to make a living. In those days, there were no backhoes. Gravel had to be shoveled and scooped into trucks by hand. Aubrey hauled gravel to the Red River Arsenal near Texarkana where military ammunition was stored—he did that until the arsenal supervisors realized that the brakes didn't work very well on two of Aubrey's trucks and they feared he might crash into one of the buildings and blow everyone up. Aubrey had also tried hauling cattle to the Fort Worth stockyards, but that hadn't been very profitable either.

I wasn't in on that first deal, but I was on the premises. Aubrey and Pat allowed me to have an "office" in the back storeroom. My desk was a plank of wood that rested on two sawhorses, and I had a phone. I used that office to take over what had been Aubrey's trucking business. I arranged various jobs that mostly related to hauling gravel from gravel pits to construction sites, many of which were in the local area. We also used our two gravel trucks—a 1940 Chevrolet and a 1936 Ford—to haul and spread gravel on Pittsburg driveways for the going price of $6 for a three-yard load, dumped and spread. In those days, most East Texans could not afford concrete and asphalt for residential driveways. A gravel driveway was the norm.

I also drove a truck for the feed store at a wage of fifty cents an hour—driving a 1945 Diamond "T" tractor with a 1946 Nabors trailer. We still have that twenty-eight-foot, single-axle trailer in our possession.

There was nothing remotely close to a long-range plan, a strategic plan, or a business plan associated with Farmer's Feed and Seed Co. I doubt if there was even very much time for daydreaming about a future. We were working long hours, sometimes hauling a load of peas over to the Cass County Canning Co. in Atlanta, Texas, not getting home until three o'clock in the morning, then getting to the store to open it at seven o'clock. Aubrey's wife, Doris, who remembers those days well, once said about my brother, "He was too busy to get very excited."

The fact is, it was all about survival.

Survival meant keeping the trucks in repair, which seemed to be almost a full-time job.

Survival meant doing extra things that had nothing to do with the price of feed or seed, such as sorting through stacks of SunGlo feed sacks to find one with a flower-print pattern that matched what a customer had purchased previously—because the end goal for that customer was to make an item of clothing for the family from the sacks.

Survival meant meeting a customer's expectations so the customer would become a *return* customer.

And in many ways, survival is not a bad approach to take in launching any business.

Seizing an Opportunity

The early partnership between my brother Aubrey and Pat Johns didn't last long. Pat decided he wanted to sell out after the first year. He didn't like worrying about the debt and was happier outside doing agricultural work and driving a truck. In fact, when he sold out his half, he retained a truck from the feed store partnership.

After Pat announced he was leaving, Aubrey asked me if I wanted to join him in the feed and seed store operation. I had already thought some about that so my answer was quick and simple: "Yes, I do."

My friend Reggie Wallace, who worked with me for more than fifty years, once recalled, "all we had in the beginning were a two-wheel buggy, a shovel, some burlap sacks, and Bo's big ideas." Most of my ideas at the beginning were about selling. I didn't know any more than Aubrey knew about feed and seed, but I did know a little about selling goods and services to people in the area. We ran dump trucks, and we sold fertilizer, plows, harnesses, and some tractor parts. We sold feed—not only for chickens, but also for hogs, dairy cows, horses, and mules. We had a little pen for live chicks that people purchased and raised solely for their table use.

I also had a desire to see things work in a more coordinated, efficient, and productive manner. The same perspective that I had as a little boy building a wagon to haul Coca-Colas to the gin found an opportunity for expression at the feed and seed store. The first year I was with my brother as a partner we added a warehouse to the store and, with it, a loading ramp, unloading pit, an elevator to carry feed to a bagging machine, and an electric sewing machine for the feed sacks. I was especially proud of the innovations we were making because much of the elevator and bagging machine design was my idea. The engineering aspect of my personality and ability had found an outlet.

These equipment changes allowed us to do several things. In the first place, we no longer lost grain through the cracks of the floor in our feed store.

In the second place, we could sell truckloads of feed out of the warehouse. Before we put in that first grain elevator, we had to load trucks with

My friend Reggie Wallace, who worked with me for more than fifty years, once recalled, "all we had in the beginning were a two-wheel buggy, a shovel, some burlap sacks, and Bo's big ideas."

grain one shovelful at a time. A customer would back up his truck to our truck, end to end. Then we'd get in there with a shovel and start filling feed sacks and stacking them in the empty truck. We worked until we had sacked up a truckload of grain. Three men could sack five tons an hour. The grain elevator allowed us to raise feed into bins and then let that grain spill down into the hundred-pound sacks. We discovered a tremendous savings in time and effort.

By moving the sacks of seed and feed out of the store and into the warehouse, we had room on the shelves of the store for other agricultural products, such as wire, nails, and tin.

We began to grow.

Perhaps more important, we began to grow in a way that, looking back, was a set of small but integrated steps. We didn't know at the time, of course, that our steps were linked in some way—we were simply responding to one opportunity after the next. In retrospect, the pieces of a fairly elaborate puzzle were beginning to fall into place.

SMALL BUT INTEGRATED STEPS

It may be helpful for you at this point to have a little better picture of the overall growing and production process related to the poultry industry. It goes like this:

- Breeder pullets, purchased from primary breeder facilities, grow up to become breeder stock.
- Parent breeders produce hatching eggs.
- Hatcheries hatch the eggs into broiler chicks.
- Feed mills produce the feed for the breeder pullets, breeders, and broilers.
- Contract growers and company-owned farms grow the baby chicks into broilers.
- An operation known as *live haul* catches the broilers and transports them to the processing plants.
- Processing plants prepare the broilers for consumers and further processing.
- Marketing sells the products.
- A distribution operation is responsible for storing and delivering the products to the customers.

The terms *live production, farm production,* and *growout* refer to all the processes necessary to grow a chicken that is ready for processing, or all the processes that precede the processing plant.

When all of these pieces are put together into one agribusiness company, you have what is known as *vertical integration.* Lots of money, time, and effort can be saved when one company is involved in all aspects of the process.

In adding a warehouse, a grain elevator, and a bagging machine to our operation, we were taking our first small steps toward becoming a fully integrated chicken-growing business.

The vertical integration of our operation took a second leap in 1950 when, at the Chamber of Commerce's request, we purchased the Hudson Cotton Gin and converted it to a feed mill.

I heard about a flour mill in Arkadelphia, Arkansas, that had gone bankrupt and closed, so I knew that certain pieces of equipment were going to be available for a good price. Aubrey and I, however, were overextended at the local bank. We turned to Dr. L. H. Pitts, a dentist in Pittsburg, who was a bank director, and we personally borrowed $10,000 from him to establish the new feed mill.

I went to Arkadelphia and purchased two roller mills from the flour milling operation, disassembled them inside the five-story brick building, and then let them down with chain hoists linked together. We installed them in the feed mill in Pittsburg, and before long, we were crimping oats and cracking milo with one of the units. We used the other to make corn chops, which are chopped corn kernels. The mill allowed us to sell grain to other feed mixers throughout East Texas.

Many of the feed customers were people in the chicken business in Camp County. Chicken houses at that time had about three thousand chickens per house. Any one grower of chickens might expect to produce four batches of chickens a year, which meant that a typical chicken farmer was producing about 12,000 chickens a year.

Some of the chicken houses in those days were much smaller. In Pittsburg, a jeweler by the name of A. H. Skipper had one behind his home on Elm Street, as a number of people did.

To today's growers, that number of chickens and chicken houses seems absurdly small. A grower today might have a dozen chicken houses on one farm, each housing up to 20,000 chickens—a single farm can grow as many as 1 million birds a year.

For us, the feed mill was the third prong in our business—we were processing feed, we were selling feed to chicken growers, and at the store, we were supplying chicks and buying back excess chickens and eggs from growers for resale. Those elements worked together in an integrated way. We certainly didn't know the term *vertical integration* in those days—but we were starting to do it.

We were also making more and more contacts in the greater East Texas area. About the same time as the feed mill opportunity arose, I went to Texas A&M for a five-week course where I learned to classify cotton and determine the staple—the length of cotton fibers. I returned to Pittsburg and began buying and selling cotton. I share that because I want you to know that we weren't focused on our poultry efforts at that time. We were focused, however, on seeing how we might work with farmers and relate to farms and be part of a greater agribusiness company that did more than sell products in one store.

The focus on chickens and eggs came about in a very natural way— it was the next opportunity that revealed itself to us.

CHICKENS AND EGGS TAKE CENTER STAGE

Just as was the case in the creation story of the Bible, chickens came first at Pilgrim's Pride. Then egg production.

As I mentioned in the previous chapter, I first learned about chickens in my grandmother's backyard. I learned a lot just by watching chickens.

I learned that a hen would turn her eggs with her beak and also peck me if I put my hand in the coop. I learned how to feed the chickens and how to shell corn for them using a hand-cranked corn-sheller. I learned how to trade surplus chickens for items we needed. And of course, I learned a lot just by being a consumer. Our primary market for chickens was ourselves—drumsticks to go with gravy and homemade biscuits!

As part of the Farmer's Feed and Seed operation, we sold baby chicks, as well as the chicken feed for them. We developed a give-and-take relationship with a number of farmers, purchasing their excess produce for resale at the store.

How did this work?

We would sell perhaps a hundred baby chicks and a sack of feed to a customer who would take the chicks home and raise them in the backyard. He used most of the chickens for his family's needs, but brought some back to us to sell at the feed store. We turned those chickens loose in a pen near the store, and local people would purchase one of them. They'd choose the one they wanted, and then it was up to me, many times, to catch that chicken around the leg using a wire hook—it was invariably the chicken in the far corner of the pen.

Aubrey and I knew a little about what it meant to raise chickens in a chicken house. We had built our first chicken house in Pine in 1945 on the family homestead even before Aubrey got into the feed store business. The chicken house we built was small by the going standards of that time. It wasn't until the early 1950s that people began to build chicken houses to raise flocks of 3,000 chicks at a time.

For us, the feed mill was the third prong in our business—we were processing feed, we were selling feed to chicken growers, and at the store, we were supplying chicks and buying back excess chickens and eggs from growers for resale. Those elements worked together in an integrated way. We certainly didn't know the term vertical integration *in those days— but we were starting to do it.*

Since we were already in the business of buying a few excess chickens here and there from our feed store customers, it was a natural progression to buy chickens from the people who had chicken houses and haul those chickens in our trucks to the Dallas and Fort Worth areas for sale. In those days, the growers held the "title" to the chickens. We simply hauled the chickens for them and, over time, began to buy from the farmers and sell to the customers in something of a broker arrangement. We had a number of grower meetings in those days, complete with barbecue and music, so we might meet with growers and solicit their business.

In 1958 we entered what I call the "Title to the Bird Period." In other words, rather than sell chickens to our customers, we utilized contract growers to grow the baby chicks for us. We used feed supplied from our mill or, in some cases, from Purina or Quaker Oats.

Prior to this, the growers purchased their own feed and chicks, and then sold grown chickens back to us for resale to processing plants. If the grower made money, he would pay his feed bill, but if he *didn't* make any money, we were left to carry the burden of his bill. We decided it was better to own the feed and the chickens rather than to take that risk.

The deal worked well for the growers too. They had a job in which a lot of the guesswork was taken out of their operation. We provided the feed, the chicks, and over time, the expertise about best management practices—from the temperature of the chicken houses to the schedule of production—all of which made for a win-win situation for the growers and for us.

This shift in our business meant that we were not only in the feedmill and feed-sales business, but also in the chicken-growing and chicken-hauling business.

The growers with whom we established agreements were quick to expand, and it seemed that overnight we faced a problem in supplying chicks to our satellite farms. Initially, we were buying chicks for the feed store from Swift and other hatcheries. They were unable to meet our growing demand for birds, however. A man named Chemmell, who had hatcheries across the United States, opened a hatchery in Mount Pleasant that went broke. Aubrey and I bought the operation in 1958 and brought in a man named James Dennis to operate it. That was our entrance to the hatchery business—and it set us up to be able to "own" a chicken from egg to processing plant.

We moved the hatchery to Pittsburg and made it part of our feed store at our new location on Market Street. We had purchased this larger facility from the Magnolia Grocery Co., and it still houses the Pilgrim's Pride Farm Supply store today.

Just as we were learning more about the hatching and growing of chickens, we also were getting a crash course in the selling of chickens. We were learning to whom we could sell, how to sell, and how to get the best price for different breeds and sizes of chickens. We sold a number of our chickens to processing plants in Terrell, Corsicana, and Paris—all towns in Texas. We also sold live birds to customers in larger cities in Texas.

The relationships we established in the 1950s with chicken growers continue to this day. Many of our contract growers have been raising our birds for years, and this now extends into the next generation, preserving the family farm. We are always adding new growers as well.

For years, a primary source of agricultural income in East Texas was dairy farming. Today, however, much of the area's milk is produced on relatively few large dairy farms. Operating a small dairy farm became difficult economically. Some dairy farmers simply retired. Some began to grow chickens for us.

Today, we supply the chicks, feed, veterinary services, and technical support to our contract growers. They provide facilities, utilities, and labor. Some are primarily breeding operations—hatching chicks. Some are primarily growout operations—raising chicks to maturity.

AND WHAT ABOUT THE EGGS?

I mentioned earlier that we bought the excess chickens from our customers. And in some cases, we bought excess eggs. We sold eggs directly to our customers and also to a broker.

One of our first customers was Billy Garrett, who had opened Mount Pleasant Poultry and Egg. Billy had chicken coops on his truck and a regular route. He'd come by and purchase excess chickens and eggs. Sometimes we'd wrestle for a dollar if he had time.

MEANWHILE, BACK AT THE FEED MILL . . .

Although we were expanding into the live production of chickens and the selling of eggs, chickens were still not our primary interest.

We were also serving the dairy industry of Northeast Texas and sold large quantities of corn, milo, cotton seed, and various other seeds, and we were the distributor for International fertilizers. The main economic base of Camp County was still cattle and row crop farming in those days, and we served primarily those farmers. A number of Pittsburg residents lived in town but owned farms outside the city limits. Others were rural resident farmers. Everybody, it seemed, had some connection to the land.

As we expanded the feed mill and storage tanks, we began to market ourselves to about a fifty-mile radius of Pittsburg, and eventually our growth attracted the attention of various officials and research groups from Texas A&M University. The feed store was located in Pittsburg, but not limited to Pittsburg. A regional trend for our operation had taken hold, almost without our knowing it.

AND THEN CAME THE DRAFT

Life changed dramatically for me in May of 1951 when I was drafted into military service. I fully expected to be sent to the front lines of the Korean War. Instead, I was shipped to California where I was selected for a leadership school for pre-officers' training. There were ninety-five men in my class, but only twenty-one of us graduated. I had a high ranking in the class, and I was assigned to remain at the school to train other draftees.

While I was in California, I saw the bulk feed trucks and large mills in use on the West Coast. I had never seen anything like these operations, and I could hardly wait to get back to Texas to tell Aubrey about all that could be done.

When I returned from army service in 1953, we installed our first three large grain tanks. The units were twenty-four feet high, fifteen feet in diameter, and each had the capacity of approximately fifteen truckloads of grain. We began to stock an inventory of corn, milo, and oats.

We also acquired our first bulk feed truck, which was the first of its kind ever used in Texas, east of Fort Worth. These trucks allowed us to supply feed directly into a grower's feed bins without the use of sacks. The truck attracted a large number of dairy and poultry grower customers who found they were able to save money and avoid the back-breaking labor of lifting hundred-pound bags of feed.

One of our first customers was Billy Garrett, who had opened Mount Pleasant Poultry and Egg. Billy had chicken coops on his truck and a regular route. He'd come by and purchase excess chickens and eggs. Sometimes we'd wrestle for a dollar if he had time.

Not long after, in 1955, we installed the first small railroad siding next to the mill. At the time, the railroad was operated by the Louisiana and Arkansas Railroad Company. I began negotiating with Paul Sipple, who was the senior vice president of the railroad and its negotiating officer. He didn't believe we could sell enough feed to justify a siding, but in the end, I proposed that we have a partnership to pay for it. We would put up some of the money, and over a period of years, the railroad could pay us back with a "per rail car" rebate fee. That worked well, and we both benefited.

As our business grew, we needed additional storage for grain. We couldn't find anybody to finance that operation, so I worked with Darryl Manley of Briggs-Weaver Machinery Co. of Dallas on a deal that resulted in our acquiring six sixty-four-foot-high Butler grain tanks at 100 percent financing. These tanks allowed us to become very aggressive in merchandising our ground milo and corn, as well as crimped items, and to begin to develop other feed mixes. A new mixing system was added to the mill in 1956.

In addition to selling to farmers, we sold grain to grocery stores and other feed dealers in nearby towns—mostly milo in those days. We received a certificate of merit from Purina for "Outstanding Retail Sales" by reaching the 50,000 ton total in the sale of Purina Chows. Another honor came to us in 1961 when The Quaker Oats Company recognized Pilgrim Feed Mills for selling more than 4,500 tons of Ful-O-Pep Feeds in a year.

Today, two railroads serve the Pilgrim's Pride feed mill in Pittsburg that is still functioning at the same location. In 1990 we expanded our railroad siding to allow us to bring in trainload deliveries of up to one hundred cars directly from the corn belt to the feed mill. This improvement in rail delivery was designed for trains arriving on the Kansas City Southern and the Union Pacific (formerly Cotton Belt) railroads.

Over the years, the mill has greatly expanded and has been modernized a number of times. Our newest expansion went on line in July 1991. The technology was the latest, and the production capacity was increased. It positioned us to produce high-quality feed for optimum chicken production at a rate of more than 120 tons an hour. It also improved the quality of all feed produced by the milling operation—it was amazing to see the computers batching various feed ingredients together. Computers also controlled everything from the monitoring of the levels in the storage bins and production hoppers, to the addition of microingredients, to the amount of steam injected during the processing.

The January 1992 issue of *Feed Management* magazine stated that the mill was called the "granddaddy" of all feed mills. Today, we move 23,000 tons of finished feed a week through that mill. Grain can be unloaded at a rate of 1,200 tons an hour. The mill today has 75 Partners working around the clock, and it has state-of-the-art safety and backup systems to assure dependable production in large quantities.

I doubt if you can calculate all the ways a bag of chicken feed might be mixed, but I suspect the number would be astronomical. Even the slightest change in ingredients can affect the performance or health of a flock. People talk about chickens as part of good nutrition for human beings. From a producer's viewpoint, the nutrition of chickens is of vital importance!

In our feed mill operation, we began to work with Dr. James Miner as our foremost nutritionist. He made the vast majority of our feed formulas through the years. There were times when various experts were in disagreement about how best to produce a desired result, so we created our own feed formulas, subjected them to tests, and manufactured the formulas.

Gone are the days when chicken feed was . . . well, just chicken feed. We have more than 250 different formulas produced on a least-cost basis that have been specifically designed to handle the nutritional needs of young chickens, pullets, and breeders at various stages of their development.

Today, in all of our feed mills combined, we produce more than 8 million tons of finished feed a year.

Gone are the days when chicken feed was . . . well, just chicken feed. We have more than 250 different formulas produced on a least-cost basis that have been specifically designed to handle the nutritional needs of young chickens, pullets, and breeders at various stages of their development.

In addition to the chicken formulas, we sell more than 1,500 tons of bulk dairy and beef feed a week, and we supply bagged feed for our own retail store. We manufacture more than 155,000 tons of high-quality bulk and bagged feed per year for livestock and show animals. The commercial feed division employs about a hundred people and has annual sales of more than $28 million.

Up to 1992, we marketed our feed under the name VIT-A-MIX, but today, all of our manufactured feed is sold as Pilgrim's Feed.

We still have a farm supply store. It sells beef, dairy, swine, horse, and dog foods; seeds; farm supplies and implements; animal medications and supplies; wire; leather goods; and hardware—in both wholesale and retail operations that serve customers throughout Northeast Texas.

We never abandoned our first business—we simply added to it!

But I'm getting ahead of myself. I must stop talking business right here and mention something even more important that happened during this time. Second only to my decision to follow Christ Jesus was my decision to marry Patty Redding, who has been my wife now for more than 49 years.

Three years after leaving the military, I began to think seriously about getting married. I began to pray for God to give me a pure, godly wife.

At the same time, I had a growing awareness that I needed to change certain aspects of my life if I was going to be in a position to deserve and win the heart of a pure young woman, so I set myself to make those changes. I stopped doing some things, started doing other things, and generally began to prepare myself mentally and emotionally for what it would mean to be a husband.

Not long after I made these changes, I met Patty. I had no doubt, and still have no doubt, that she was God-sent to me. She was an answer to prayer. I'll have more to say later about how we met and about our family life. One thing is certain: There is no way I could have accomplished what I have in my life without Patty by my side.

As Your Business
Grows and Expands

In the 1950s in our company, there was still one more step we needed to take to have a fully vertically integrated operation. That was to prove the most challenging step—and it remains the area in which we face the greatest opportunities today: processing and prepared foods (fully cooked or ready-to-cook chicken products).

I don't know what business you may be in, but as you expand, I encourage you to consider these three lessons from my experience:

First, as good as a long-range strategic plan may be as you envision your business and its expansion—or perhaps as you envision your personal career—don't allow yourself to get bogged down by your plan. Businesses, as well as careers, tend to expand in the direction of opportunity. Seize the good opportunities that come your way. Don't delay. Have a criterion for determining whether an opportunity has merit, and once you draw the conclusion that it does, take action.

As good as a long-range strategic plan may be as you envision your business and its expansion—or perhaps as you envision your personal career— don't allow yourself to get bogged down by your plan. Businesses, as well as careers, tend to expand in the direction of opportunity.

Second, seek to coordinate your various enterprises as you expand. Weigh opportunities on the basis of how each opportunity fits into the greater whole. Our business expanded on many different fronts, but each front was an extension of something we were already doing. Recognize that the expansion of a career or a business is far more organic—like a living, growing organism—than mechanical. Expansion is often *not* in an orderly pattern of same-sized increments.

Third, trust God to do the overall orchestrating of your master plan. God took me from hauling gravel to hauling feed to selling feed. From there, He led us to growing the chickens that were consuming the feed, and then to selling the chickens and hatching their replacements. The more chickens we grew, the more we needed additional feed. The more sales of feed we were able to produce with added technology and upgraded equipment, the greater the contacts we had with growers who might want to raise chickens.

My point is this: every aspect of our business is in some way linked to every other aspect. Could we see the big picture of this as we were working sixteen hours a day, scrambling to make the next deal, work out the details of the next sale, or meet the next customer demand? No. But we trusted in the One who could see the beginning from the ending.

God knows how to grow your business in ways you can't imagine.

God knows how to coordinate your business in ways you can't fathom.

God knows how to orchestrate the overall plan in ways you can't predict or control.

Trust Him. And do the work that He puts immediately in front of you to do.

★ ★ ★

The steps of a good man are ordered by the LORD,
And He delights in his way.
(Ps. 37:23 NKJV)

3

THIS LITTLE CHICKEN
WENT TO MARKET . . .

The processing of chickens was the final link for us.

In 1957 a group of businessmen in Titus, Morris, and Upshur Counties obtained a Small Business Administration loan to build a chicken processing plant in Mount Pleasant, Texas, which is just about ten miles north of Pittsburg, where we were located. After two years of operating the plant unsuccessfully, they leased it to Ray Climber of Tyler. He ran the company for a year, but also was unsuccessful. In 1960 Aubrey and I took the risk of operating the processing plant—we were determined *not* to fail!

It was a calculated risk. We had been watching what was going on in the poultry business in other parts of the United States, and we had a strong vision for a fully integrated poultry operation, which included processing the chickens we were growing.

Our financiers, however, didn't share our confidence.

At the time, we were financing chickens through Marshall Production Credit Association, and the management there would not approve our expansion. The managers threatened to withdraw our credit line if we pursued the lease of the plant.

We went on a secret mission. Aubrey and I went ahead and leased the plant and, at the same time, hired a man by the name of Sam Hatcher to manage the operation—all without any reference to us. Hatcher had previously been employed at a processing plant in Terrell, Texas, and at a turkey processing plant in California. The citizens of Mount Pleasant and Pittsburg, including our bankers, assumed that Hatcher owned the plant. They didn't know he was working for us for a salary and percentage of the profits.

One thing that had kept the previous plants from being profitable was a shortage of live chickens to process. Even though we had utilized a number of growers to produce chickens for us, we needed more chickens to overcome this shortage. We purchased additional chicks over the telephone on a weekly basis from a live chicken auction. The auction was conducted from an office in Center, Texas. Every week, we received a list of chicken growers in East and South Texas—the list included the location of the grower, the number of chickens he had available for sale, the size of the chickens, and their breed. A telephone conference call allowed several buyers to be on the line simultaneously bidding for the chickens of their choice. Once a buyer had made a purchase, it was the buyer's responsibility to pick up the chickens or contract to have them picked up. The grower had to furnish the catchers—in other words, get the chickens onto the truck.

Aubrey and I, of course, couldn't be involved directly in these auctions—if we had been, our cover would have been blown. The financing for Sam Hatcher to buy the chickens was made under the company name of Netex Poultry Company, with money provided through a bank in Mount Pleasant. The live chickens were financed in individual farmers' notes by the First National Bank of Mount Pleasant. After the chickens were sold, Aubrey and I paid off the farmers' notes.

This went on for a couple of years, but by the end of 1961, the operation was successful and the processing plant was openly operated as Pilgrim Poultry Co.

LOOKING WEST

Much of our processed product was shipped to the West.

There are a lot more chicken processors in the eastern half of the

United States—but as Texans, we've always been encouraged to "think west" and to take full advantage of our ability to have a significant marketing impact in that direction. Although we didn't really plan it to be this way, our fresh chicken—for foodservice and retail accounts—was distributed primarily west of the Mississippi until just a few years ago.

The main chicken products we sold in the first several decades of our business were these:

- Fresh chicken to fast-food and other national restaurant chains
- Ice-pack chicken to distributors
- Eggs to foodservice and independent grocers

VERTICAL INTEGRATION HAD TAKEN HOLD!

By the time the prosperous 1980s were beginning, we were a fully integrated chicken producer and a major commercial egg producer. We had two hatcheries, three processing plants, and two feed mills, and we owned a poultry and egg marketing and distribution division. We were creating our own feed formulas.

We were well diversified in agribusiness—we had twenty-eight company-owned farms, a farm-supply division, and a cattle operation located on 2,700 acres of owned and leased land.

By 1981, annual production had reached 234 million pounds of dressed poultry and 34 million dozen table eggs.

On the financial side, vertical integration was allowing us to control schedules and costs from top to bottom and, more important, to control the level of quality and service we could provide. By coordinating every tier of our organization, we were able to provide the best possible value to our customers.

Increasingly we turned to our customers to tell us what they wanted.

We were not product-driven. We were customer-driven. What our customers wanted, we did our best to provide.

In 1986 we began to produce lines of further-processed cooked chicken and deli products in a new state-of-the-art production facility in Mount Pleasant, Texas. Today, this facility has 275,000 square feet and is a Prepared Foods plant. It is located next to what we call the East Plant, which provides us a continuous flow of fresh chicken. Located on the same property, the West Plant became devoted to supplying an additional 1.6 million birds a week to Prepared Foods.

On the financial side, vertical integration was allowing us to control schedules and costs from top to bottom and, more important, to control the level of quality and service we could provide. By coordinating every tier of our organization, we were able to provide the best possible value to our customers.

The Prepared Foods plant in Mount Pleasant is one of the most advanced of its kind in the United States. I've always been a firm believer that if a particular piece of equipment or a system could give us better flexibility and quality, we needed to acquire that equipment or system.

The plant originally had a capacity of two 4,000-pounds-an-hour formed product lines. We could run individually quick frozen (IQF) deboned products and bone-in, fully cooked or ready-to-cook products.

We quickly expanded by adding two additional lines in 1987. Today, this facility has eight lines and sixteen deboning and portioning lines. We now debone more than 6 million pounds of chicken a week in that plant. This has provided employment for about 2,000 people and has become one of our most productive operations.

We opened a facility in Pittsburg in 2002 that functions as a 155,000-square-foot receiving and distribution center for frozen foods. We have robotic technology to handle customer orders in sequence of delivery.

This one center holds enough chicken to feed half of the U.S. population a chicken sandwich. Think about it. That's a *lot* of chicken.

THE TREND TOWARD PREPARED FOODS

The overall progression of our company reveals the trend that shapes much of what we do today:

In the 1940s, we sold grain to feed chickens.

In the 1950s, we sold live chickens.

In the 1960s, we sold ice-packed chicken in wooden crates.

In the 1980s, we sold chill-pack chicken (fresh, prepackaged chicken).

In the 1990s, we began to sell fully cooked, portion-controlled products.

The nation was moving at the same time toward an increased customer demand for quick-to-fix, ready-to-eat products. Americans wanted high-quality food that required less cooking time, less preparation time, and less planning time. That trend continues today.

In the period of 1990–92 alone, our research and development (R & D) department created 160 new products, which represented about 30 percent of our total volume by 1992. The new categories that really took off were the nonbreaded, nonfried, healthy products.

The world has seemed a little slow in coming around to the concept of healthy meat products, although fine dining has always been in style and there's nothing that can beat good ol' home cooking of fresh produce, dairy products, and meat. Our society has a growing desire, it seems, to have everything faster and better.

A significant percentage of our chicken products are sold in a ready-to-eat form to national quick-service chain restaurants. We sell chicken products to more than 70 percent of the top fifty U.S. foodservice companies. We also market our products to supermarkets and club stores.

Through the years, we have done very well with our chicken nuggets, patties, and other convenience cooked products. Our goal is to put products on the market that have nothing artificial about them—the food is lean, nutritious, and without preservatives or additives.

I should also admit this. In the mid-to-late 1980s when we first established the deli business at Pilgrim's Pride—with sliced chicken, all-chicken franks and bologna, and so forth—the product line did *not* yield for us the profit margin we desired. Our customers, it seemed, wanted chicken that came in chunks of some type—nuggets, tenders (filets), and so forth.

At the time we opened the Prepared Foods plant, I knew that there were some people in our industry who were a bit skeptical. They didn't think we had customers committed to buying our products before we started building the plant, and that's something of a corporate no-no. That's not my style, however. I had a very strong conviction that people in the United States were going to want more and more variety in their chicken products, and that they would be consuming an increasing amount of chicken as the years went by.

I might not have been right about some of the deli items, but I was definitely right on the variety and volume issues.

I was also right in making sure that whatever system we implemented had flexibility so that we could expand and change if necessary, without any loss of quality or efficiency. I have absolutely no doubt that if a company can act quickly on its formulations and reformulations, and rapidly change product lines to meet customer needs, that company can be very successful.

Since 2000, we have seen tremendous growth in our Prepared Foods Division—on average, we've experienced close to 13 percent annual growth. Prepared Foods sales now represent a little more than half of our total chicken sales. The good news for us is that the Prepared Foods segment is not as dependent on commodity-style pricing as fresh chicken.

FLEXIBILITY IS A KEY FACTOR

The Mount Pleasant facility has been designed for maximum versatility and flexibility. We debone front halves, which are produced at two adjacent processing plants. Some of these are individually quick frozen (IQF) products. We have had three major expansions of the Prepared Foods plant since 1986. Initially the facility had a two-line capacity of 8,000 pounds an hour. The plant now has eight production lines. It is a seven-day-a-week production facility that handles more than 7 million pounds of chicken a week.

The product mix is constantly changing. I don't have any doubt that the adaptability and quality of this food processing facility make it the best in the United States.

Many poultry companies use smaller plants that specialize in a single product. We rely on flexibility to adapt to new products in a larger facility, coupled with frequent upgrades in equipment. It was a major innovation when we added "slice and dice" capabilities to this plant, using robotic knives and other equipment. Again, it was a mind-boggling thing!

This Mount Pleasant plant can produce almost any type of poultry product on the market today. More than 2,000 different products roll through these production lines every year.

A CASE STUDY IN ADAPTABILITY

Apart from processes inside our various plants, we have an example of flexibility and adaptability on the front lawn of the Pittsburg freezer-distribution center, a massive facility that rises above the country skyline and can be seen from vantage points many miles away.

People who drive down Highway 271 past this distribution center are often surprised to come across a large statue that depicts my head and likeness wearing a Pilgrim hat. Few people today, however, seem to know where that statue originated.

In the late 1960s, we opened a little restaurant in Pittsburg called Pilgrim's Kitchen. A large Pilgrim hat was constructed and placed on top of the restaurant, which primarily sold fried chicken and the side dishes that are often associated with it. The hat made Pilgrim's Kitchen instantly recognizable, even from a distance.

I realized that since Pilgrim's Pride was selling chicken to virtually all of the restaurants that sold chicken in the area, we were actually competing with our own customers! So, we closed the restaurant in 2001 and focused on growing our customer base, which in the long run was a good business move on our part.

The building in which the restaurant was located was easily sold, but what to do with the hat? It was large and heavy . . . and there seemed to be no really good use for it, but it had been a highly recognizable symbol of the Pilgrim's Pride brand and it was sort of a fixture in our community. Finally someone suggested that it be put in front of our Pittsburg freezer-distribution center right along the highway—at least there it would serve an advertising purpose—but a hat sitting by itself out in the field in front of the freezer didn't seem to make much sense.

By that time, my likeness had become very well known, being seen quite often on television commercials and on our delivery vehicles that were crisscrossing the region. So, we had a likeness of my head and shoulders cast in the same material as the hat and put the hat on top of my head. Many people have told me that they knew instantly that they were looking at a Pilgrim's Pride business when they saw the statue—even before they read the name on the building.

The head statue was *not* an ego trip for me, as some have assumed. It was just an effective and fun way to help publicize Pilgrim's Pride to thousands of potential customers driving by on a busy Texas highway. Our company's senior management team even commissioned a famous artist to create a sculpture of me holding my Bible, that now sits in a pavilion under the hat and my head.

The Goal of Adding Value

In the early years, we added value to our products through vertical integration that gave us greater quality control and allowed us to provide better customer service. Today, we add value through leading-edge further-processing and innovative new products.

These days, we aren't as concerned about additional growth in tonnage; rather, we increase profits through value-added products—the market segments in our industry known as prepared foods, retail-branded chill pack, and fast foods. The math is really very simple: if a customer asks you to give him a whole five-pound chicken at seventy cents a pound, that's a $3.50 sale for one bird. But if the customer asks you to give him two chicken breasts marinated and vacuum packed in portion-controlled packaging and he's willing to pay $3.00 for that one item, and he asks you to give him the wings, thighs, and drumsticks barbecued and available for sale in the deli for what amounts to an average of $2.00 per chicken, that's a total sale of $5.00 for one bird. The more the processor and prepared foods supplier does, the greater the potential profit margin, and the more value for the product in the eyes of the person buying the item.

What might this mean to you in your business or career?

Versatility.

Flexibility.

Adaptability.

These are the key concepts for staying on the cutting edge of any business. Your business plan needs versatility built into it so you can add and subtract products quickly to meet ever-changing customer needs.

The people at every level of your organization—from upper management to line workers—have to be flexible. Even if you are in a solo career, you need to associate with people who are flexible in their thinking, quick to adapt to trends and demands.

Your equipment and processes need to be adaptable and easily adjusted for multiple functions. That's the wave of the future.

Above all, every person in business today faces the challenge of being innovative—of using innovative technology and new processes, and coming up with new products or new features for old ones.

There's only one Creator. All ideas flow from Him. All innovation comes about at His inspiration. Ask Him to help you.

★   ★   ★

All things come from You,
And of Your own we have given You.
(1 Chron. 29:14 NKJV)

4

CHICKEN IS SOMETHING TO CROW ABOUT!

A young businessperson who dreamed of really making a mark in this world—and who specifically dreamed of starting and developing a big company—once asked me what I considered to be the business cornerstone that needed to be laid in order to establish a solid foundation for growth. I told him that he needed to focus on his first product. Specifically he needed to find a product that was good for people—and that people liked. The product needed to be versatile and have good expansion possibilities.

"Like what?" this young person asked.

"Well," I said as I thought for a moment, "like chicken!"

Chicken has it all.

CHICKEN IS GOOD FOR PEOPLE— AND THEY LIKE IT!

There's nothing that can beat chicken when it comes to high nutritional value—plenty of high-quality protein for minimal expense. Unlike fattier red meats—beef, pork, and even lamb—chicken that is grilled without the skin and with all excess fat trimmed away is an extremely lean source of protein. It has great value economically. A pound of chicken still costs significantly less than a pound of red meat. Chicken consumption, per capita on a retail weight basis, is the number one meat in the United States today, according to the United States Department of Agriculture. Chicken consumption surpassed beef consumption in 1992 and is still climbing!

In my lifetime, chicken has grown from a poor man's food to the preferred meat of the world. Chicken is the favorite protein for Americans, whether eating out or at home. The same is true for children today—they *choose* chicken. As the baby boomers approach retirement, chicken's health benefits seem even more attractive to them.

I believe chicken will remain the preferred meat of the future. Nothing beats chicken in cost, taste, and nutritional value. The world might have been a little slow coming around to that realization, but the truth eventually wins out.

Chicken Is Versatile

Versatility can be defined in many ways. From one perspective, chicken is versatile because no part of the chicken is wasted.

Feathers and viscera are processed into quality pet food product ingredients. Most people don't realize it, but feathers are extremely rich in protein.

Leg quarters are frozen for export markets around the globe.

Chicken feet, which are called *paws,* are sold to Asian markets.

From a second perspective, chicken has been shown to be versatile over the years when it comes to the consumer market. We started out selling live chickens. Then we had to take the feathers off. Then we had to cut up the chicken and sell the pieces because some people wanted only breasts, others only thighs, and some only legs. Then we had to cook the chickens—and do so in lots of different ways. Change has been the nature of our business from the first day to today, but chicken has been a product that could be *changed* to meet consumer demands.

From yet a third perspective, chicken is versatile in the number of ways it can be prepared. Years ago, just about everybody roasted or fried chicken. Now you can go into any large grocery deli and find a wide variety of chicken products—there are fried chickens, fried chicken tenders, rotisserie chicken, baked chicken, barbecued chicken, regular wings, hot wings, honey barbecued wings, chicken salad, chicken loaf, processed chicken that can be sliced or shredded to a customer's specifications, and usually a variety of other salads that have chicken added to them—from oriental salads to Caesar salads to pasta salads. Chicken is one of the most versatile foods in the world.

CHICKEN HAS ENJOYED TREMENDOUS GROWTH POTENTIAL

Through the years, the amount of chicken we consume as Americans has risen fairly steadily. In 1950, Americans ate an average of twenty pounds of chicken a year. At the beginning of the twenty-first century, we were eating almost ninety pounds of chicken per year! And we are paying less per pound at the supermarket for chicken than fifty years ago. Advances in farming, processing, and marketing technologies have made the difference.

Consumption of pork has been relatively flat for the last decade, and beef consumption has declined, but chicken consumption has shot upward. In fact, since 1975 the per capita consumption of chicken in the United States has more than doubled. Egg consumption has also risen, although not as rapidly.

International forecasting trends indicate that consumption of chicken will also continue to grow in Eastern Europe, Korea, China, the Middle East, Latin America, and other areas of the world.

Some people I know eat a portion of chicken every day—I'm one of them, of course. At that rate, assuming each portion is about six ounces, a person might easily eat more than 150 pounds of chicken in a year!

Overall, the chicken industry has enjoyed an incredibly consistent annual growth rate in production of about 5 percent. This relatively steady pace has been sustained for more than 40 years.

In 1960, the U.S. chicken industry was producing less than 5 billion pounds of chicken products a year. By the mid-1990s, the industry was at 25 billion pounds a year. Today, the number has topped 33 billion.

In simple terms, people are continuing to eat more and more chicken.

MAXIMIZING THE HEALTH POTENTIAL

The challenge, of course, that faces a company that has a product with such tremendous likability, versatility, and growth potential is this: How can you make the product even better? In our case, the challenge was finding ways to make the product better by making it healthier.

In 1963 my brother Aubrey suffered his first heart attack, and as he recovered, he insisted that we sell the company to Quaker Oats. It took a hard sell on my part, but I eventually talked him out of that idea. Aubrey recovered, he resumed his duties, and we continued to grow.

Then in 1966 Aubrey's health problems resurfaced. He felt a great deal of stress after a poultry trucking accident took the lives of several of his close friends. He died of a heart attack on November 11, 1966.

At the time Aubrey died, we had been in business together for twenty years. The company did about $10.5 million in annual sales. We had pretty much divided up our partner roles. Aubrey was in charge of sales, customer service, financing, and the hatchery operation. I was in charge of feed manufacturing, purchasing, nutrition, and transportation.

I can't begin to tell you what a shock Aubrey's death was to me. My whole world was shaken.

On the other hand, I was well aware of the terrible health history of our family, especially when it came to heart problems. My grandfather D. D. Pilgrim died at the age of 49. My father died when he was 44. My brother Harold Dean died at age 59. My brother Billy Carroll died at age

46, my sister Mary Katheryn Pilgrim at age 39, and my brother Aubrey at age 42. Most of my siblings who died young died of heart ailments. Arteriosclerosis—more commonly known as hardening of the arteries—is common in my family.

I had open-heart surgery in 1975 to deal with some coronary blockages. In 1982 I had a mild heart attack. These health problems were certainly in keeping with my overall family history—which I admit I largely ignored. These heart incidents in my life could have been setbacks in my life and career, but I chose to make them stepping-stones. I began a diligent personal campaign to live healthier and to eat more nutritiously. I also became extremely dedicated to seeing that our company create healthier, more nutritious chicken products.

In 1984, we developed the first lean chicken, which had less fat and cholesterol, no artificial color pigments, and fewer calories.

In 1997, we developed nutritionally enhanced eggs with omega-3, omega-6 fatty acids, and vitamin E. They are marketed under the EggsPlus™ brand.

A person asked me not too long ago, "How can you make a chicken leaner and eggs more nutritious?" It's all a matter of what a chicken is fed. The EggsPlus eggs were created by feeding laying hens a grain-based diet that was enhanced with fish oil, flaxseed, vitamin E, and lutein. The result is that two EggsPlus™ eggs provide the same amount of omega-3 as a serving of salmon, and seven times more vitamin E than regular eggs.

Chicken and eggs were already products with good health value. We turned them into products with *great* health value.

PROMOTE YOUR WAY TO THE TOP

If you have a good product that you have made even better, that's something to crow about! There's no substitute for letting the world know what you have so the world can beat a path to your door.

I mentioned versatility earlier, and when it comes to promoting chicken as a product, there's tremendous versatility in what can be said about chicken—and in a creative way. There are dozens of good phrases that make for good headlines. Here are just three of my favorites:

- Families Flock to Chicken Dinner
- Company Stays Abreast of Chicken-Product Trends
- New Products Are Winging Their Way Out of the Deli

Commercials have been essential to our growth. The benefit of a commercial is that you can tell the benefits of your product, differentiate yourself from your competition, build pride in your organization, and create a heightened image with suppliers and customers—all in ten to thirty seconds at a time.

Our advertising began in earnest in the early 1980s. In late 1982 I went with Don Perkins, our senior vice president of processing and marketing, and Buddy Pilgrim, our director of marketing, to interview about a dozen advertising agencies in Dallas. We finally selected KCBN Advertising to develop our company's first consumer ads to introduce our new line of fresh chill-pack chicken. KCBN went through several name changes over the years, and it eventually became the Evans Group. It was our advertising agency for six years. The Richards Group, another well-respected Dallas company, became our agency of record in 1989. Today, it is The Wolf Agency in Dallas.

I was the logical spokesperson for the company in our first TV commercial, titled "The President Speaks," which aired in early 1983. I actually volunteered for this role as spokesperson because I knew that nobody knew our products, our company, our potential customers, or the benefits of our products better than I did. Furthermore, it was my name on the company. In those days especially, a number of advertising campaigns featured the owner or president of the company doing the advertising—I saw it as a mark of integrity for us. I wasn't about to say anything over the public airwaves that I wasn't fully prepared to deliver to the customers.

People seemed to like my dry wit, so I had something of a permanent job for all subsequent TV and radio commercials. I put on a business suit and then donned a black buckled Pilgrim hat on my white hair. With a name like Pilgrim, what could be more logical? And what could be more appropriate than to have this image front and center stage for the two biggest holidays of the year—Thanksgiving and Christmas? They just happen to be feast days that are known for poultry consumption.

We also adopted Henrietta. I had gone to San Francisco to make one of our first television commercials, and on Sunday night before the shooting of the commercial, a group of us went out to dinner. I had a chicken that had made a trip to a taxidermist sitting on the table at the restaurant with us, and a man came by and said, "That looks like Henrietta"—which I learned later was a character in a children's book. The name stuck, and I began to carry that stuffed chicken named Henrietta with me not only in commercials, but every time I put on the Pilgrim hat for public appearances.

One person said to me not long ago, "You stood out in a way that we could remember both you and what you were selling." He said I represented a rare blend of personality, product, and product name. Over the years, experts in advertising have told me that I am something of a folk hero to millions of people through our award-winning advertisements. We eventually put the image of me wearing the hat on our company trucks as a way of extending our advertising on the open roads. It worked.

I worked hard at promoting the company and being its number one booster. The advertising and promotional effort was not just a matter of doing a couple of commercials for a few hours in any given year. I made promotional appearances and gave more after-dinner speeches than I can begin to count. I also appeared on television and radio talk shows and did interviews with newspaper and magazine editors.

PROMOTING YOUR INNOVATIONS

I have always looked for ways of doing things better or in a more innovative way. That's true when it comes to chicken as well as other things.

A milestone for our company, and our corporate image, came in 1984 when I took on the challenge of creating a whole boneless chicken. The challenge was issued to me by Dick Yaws, a farm radio reporter. At the time, we were discussing how to cut up a chicken, and the conversation turned to how to debone a chicken. I went on television later, talked about how to debone a chicken, and then deboned a whole chicken.

I had worked dozens of nights over several months to experiment with various techniques until I had perfected my method. The end result was the removal of all bones from a whole chicken without any additional incisions other than those originally used in processing.

One person said to me not long ago, "You stood out in a way that we could remember both you and what you were selling."

People seemed fascinated with the concept of a whole boneless chicken, and I was interviewed by numerous writers from magazines and newspapers, including the editors of *Good Housekeeping* magazine, about the process. The whole boneless chicken not only added to our exposure, but also took us into the realm of being perceived as a serious innovator of quality food products.

It's not often that a unique new meat product appears on the market—the whole boneless chicken was such a product. We received major recognition from as far away as London. Not only were the mass media intrigued with the idea, but also the food-related magazines and food buyers. Across America, the Pilgrim's Pride label had a huge boost in recognition. Production at the De Queen, Arkansas, plant had to increase dramatically—at the time, it was the only place we were producing boneless chicken.

I termed the whole boneless chicken product "a mind-boggling thing." That was the first time I used that phrase—it subsequently became something of a theme for us and eventually became a catchphrase across the United States.

CHICKEN AS "CUISINE"

Part of my motivation for creating boneless chicken came from an article I read in the 1960s stating that 60 percent of the chicken that was consumed in Japan was *boneless* chicken. In my experience to that point, chicken was usually *fried* chicken, and it was considered something of a picnic food—a good dish to be eaten outdoors or on a screened-in porch. Fried chicken was also regular family fare—usually with biscuits and gravy—but chicken was rarely considered to be a food that was served to company, nor was it a meat that people ordered frequently when they were in restaurants. When I read this article about the Japanese consumption of boneless chicken, I suddenly had a whole new vision for what chicken might be as cuisine. I could see it served in fancy restaurants with white tablecloths—ordered as a preferred choice of meat over beef or pork. I could see it becoming company food, served as an entrée for special guests.

My new understanding about what chicken might be was really the beginning of a slow but steady movement toward an increased number of prepared foods—which today is a highly profitable part of our Pilgrim's Pride business. There are countless ways of preparing chicken, and we are intent on exploring the marketability of as many of them as possible. The vast majority of prepared food items, of course, use boneless chicken pieces.

The amazing thing to me is that the whole boneless chicken product didn't catch on with the consumer. It ultimately failed to capture sufficient market share, and we discontinued it. The uniqueness of the product at the time, however, generated tremendous national attention. That made it a great success.

ON TO A LEANER, NO-YELLOW CHICKEN

The whole boneless chicken campaign showed us the great importance of having innovative products. We followed up in 1985 with a promotion for leaner, natural chicken—as opposed to fat yellow chickens. Not long ago, I met a person whose first words to me were not, "Oh, hello, Bo, glad to meet you," but, "No yellow chicken!" She still remembered the message of that advertising campaign.

When I said in our commercials, "I just won't sell a fat yellow chicken," I really meant it. It wasn't an advertising gimmick. I don't say things—publicly or privately—that I don't mean. Early in my life I made a commitment to honor the Lord in all things, and that means telling the truth is one of life's nonnegotiables.

We had worked with Dr. James Miner, our nutrition expert, to produce a line of low-calorie feed that gave us chickens with less fat. We refused to add any artificial color pigments, of course. The new product was also possible because we were using younger birds and special trimming procedures.

I took to the airwaves with a very successful television commercial that promoted "guaranteed leaner chicken." And our sales force hit the road to secure new distribution outlets from Missouri to California.

The leaner chicken had immediate consumer appeal. This product came out at just the right time. Americans were increasingly concerned about fatty foods and were ready for exactly the type of product we had created.

As a result of the near immediate boost in sales and consumer demand, we sold out of processing capacity in De Queen, Arkansas, and needed more chill-pack volume. To address this situation, we purchased Pluss-Tex Poultry of Lufkin and Nacogdoches. The deal was closed in June 1985 after only six weeks of negotiation. In less than a year, we had more than doubled the capacity at the Lufkin plant to handle 850,000 birds per week.

When I said in our commercials, "I just won't sell a fat yellow chicken," I really meant it. It wasn't an advertising gimmick. I don't say things—publicly or privately—that I don't mean. Early in my life I made a commitment to honor the Lord in all things, and that means telling the truth is one of life's nonnegotiables. I'm all for advertising, but I'm even more in favor of truth in advertising.

The Texas Public Relations Association gave me an award for my role in the communications program that introduced boneless chicken to American consumers. In 1986 the Dallas/Fort Worth Chapter of the American Marketing Association named me Marketer of the Year. Awards such as these gave us something additional to crow about in our advertisements and commercials.

STAYING VISIBLE
IN MANY VENUES

As important as advertising and commercials were to our fresh chill-pack chicken in the 1980s, we didn't limit ourselves to print and television promotion. I devoted a tremendous amount of time to keeping the company and its products visible in as many venues as possible.

I never considered any audience too small. I have spoken at banquets, association functions, business meetings, club luncheons, civic club breakfasts, conventions, fund-raisers, high school classes, college seminars, church activities and stewardship-drive meetings, Rotary Club and Lions Club lunches from coast to coast, in big cities and small towns. One thing I did try to ensure was that if I was speaking to a group, club, or organization at a mealtime, the hotel or restaurant catering the event had been furnished with Pilgrim's Pride chicken. I would have considered it a major obstacle to have an audience eating steak while I was talking to them with a stuffed chicken under one arm!

Occasionally, we sponsored an event at which I spoke. For years— actually more than forty years—we sponsored a breakfast in honor of Future Farmers and 4-H council members at the annual Southwestern Exposition and Fat Stock Show in Fort Worth. It gave us an opportunity to honor young men and women we hoped would be tomorrow's agribusiness leaders.

Sometimes you're smart to create events that tie in with something you want to promote or honor. We placed a historical marker at the site of our first feed store during our fiftieth anniversary, as well as commemorative architectural plaques at our Pilgrim's Pride facilities. We certainly didn't miss the opportunity to invite state officials, local leaders, customers, employees, media, and others to the official opening or official dedication of our major facilities.

From time to time we sponsored events at which we might showcase our products. For example, we sponsored the Chef's Competition staged by the American Heart Association's Dallas Chapter one year. Our goal was to "alert and inform the public regarding a heart healthy diet." That's a code phrase for *chicken*. We promoted our new leaner chicken products at the event. Dallas-area celebrity chefs competed for prizes and created dishes from the ingredients we furnished to them, including Pilgrim's Pride chicken. The winning chefs prepared a meal—actually it was a gala dinner party that the public could attend for $150 per person, all funds donated to the American Heart Association. I was the guest speaker.

By the way, for five years the Dallas Chapter of the American Heart Association sponsored a Heart Healthy Recipe Contest. We joined with the AHA in printing and distributing thousands of winning recipe cards, at least some of which featured Pilgrim's Pride chicken.

Locally, we help sponsor the ChickFest in Pittsburg, Texas—several days of celebration that include lots of activities from horseshoe tournaments to children's competitions and always a chicken-cooking contest. The entries are innovative, and sometimes upwards of sixty recipes are judged. We give away prizes—in the $250, $500, and $1,000 range—and have fun doing it. Whenever I can, I like to ride in the parade. I ride in an old truck that is similar to the one I was paid fifty cents an hour to drive for Aubrey before I became a partner in the feed store.

We did a number of other innovative promotions in the 1980s and 1990s:

The State Fair of Texas. We worked out a deal with the State Fair of Texas to accept three specially marked labels from Pilgrim's Pride Boneless Chicken as the admission price for one adult. I made appearances in the Food Pavilion at the fair, passed out chicken chili, and gave away prizes. My favorite prize to give, of course, was always a year's supply of chicken.

The Movie Premiere. We cosponsored with Safeway the world premiere of Robert Redford's comedy-thriller *Legal Eagles* in which Debra Winger and Daryl Hannah also starred. The event was held in Dallas. Redford had to show up only at the theater and a private reception. I showed up with Henrietta at the Safeway stores.

The Texas Rangers. On another occasion, we sponsored Pilgrim's Pride "Pack the Park Night" at the Texas Rangers major-league baseball stadium in Arlington. I threw out the first pitch and cackled and strutted with the San Diego Chicken on the field, to the delight of sixty thousand fans. Pilgrim's Pride TV spots were put on the scoreboard during the game, and a promotional handout was given to fans as they arrived that night. I decided I was very grateful that nobody ever asked me to wear a chicken suit. We did, however, sponsor some events in which people were given prizes for the wackiest chicken costumes or the most hilarious chicken cackles.

The Dallas Cowboys. We didn't ignore football. When the Dallas Cowboys met the Pittsburgh Steelers in Super Bowl XXX—January 1996—we took the occasion to enter into the friendly mayoral wagering between the two cities. The Dallas mayor pledged a truckload of Pilgrim's Pride chicken should Pittsburgh win. The Pittsburgh, Pennsylvania, mayor made the *same* offer. In the end, a truckload of chicken was donated to food banks in both cities. The week of that Super Bowl, the officials in my hometown of Pittsburg, Texas, voted to officially change the name of our town for just that one week to Cowboys, Texas. The ploy won national press coverage for Pittsburg, Texas—and in turn, Pilgrim's Pride.

In every one of these marketing-related activities I saw a three-part opportunity:

First, to promote the products of our company.

Second, to send the message that it was vitally important for us at Pilgrim's Pride, and for people everywhere, to choose not to be average in whatever enterprise they found themselves.

Third, to send a spiritual message that God is the One who gives us our talents, abilities, and opportunities. Nothing happens without God's favor.

I realize that a number of people who interviewed me allowed me to express my spiritual message because I was successful financially—and perhaps also because I laced everything I said with a little dry humor. Had I not been successful in business, or had our products not been excellent, I would not have had this opportunity to share a spiritual message.

LOBBYING OUR CAUSE

There's yet another dimension of promotion that is often overlooked because it falls under the category of politics.

A columnist for the *East Texas Journal*, Hudson Old, once said that I had "more political arms than an octopus."

It wasn't always that way. There was a time when I thought politics was a waste of time and, in particular, a waste of my brother Aubrey's time. I wasn't much into politics when I first went into business with my brother. Aubrey was the one who frequently could be found in a local café with the politicians of the community, county, and state. I thought he was wasting his time—actually I thought he was goofing off by spending so much time with people who held elected office.

What I did consider to be a more legitimate form of political influence in those early days was joining professional organizations and becoming active in them. I knew intuitively that with business success in your own corporation comes a responsibility to see that all businesses associated with yours also succeed. I also recognized the truth that if the water level for your entire industry rises, your boat will rise as well! To this day, I don't limit my efforts to Pilgrim's Pride Corporation. I have spent considerable time, effort, and money in other activities that promote the poultry industry and related agricultural concerns. I believe it's very important for any company leader to be actively involved with other people who are in the same business. There's much to be gained by cooperative friendship, even if you are engaged in competitive business. I encourage young businesspeople in many fields to get to know their colleagues and to be willing to work for the good of their mutual interests and concerns.

Through the years, I have been very active in a number of organizations, such as the Midwest Feed Manufacturers Association, the Texas Water Resources Board, and the Governor's Task Force for Agriculture. I serve on the Executive Committee and the Board of Directors of the National Chicken Council in Washington, D.C.

I have found repeatedly that when one seeks to raise his own business apart from others, he tends to fail. On the other hand, when one seeks to raise the entire industry in which his business thrives, he tends to succeed—in his own business and as part of the greater whole. This has been especially true as our company has grown and expanded into foreign markets.

One of the facts of the poultry industry is that Americans prefer the white meat of chicken. That means that we've needed to look for new international markets for dark meat, which is less popular in the United States. We export about a billion pounds of poultry every year.

This, in turn, means that international politics come into play. As an example, not very long ago we were facing a serious shutout in Russia— the Russians simply weren't allowing our product into their nation, even though their people wanted chicken and had the ability to pay for it.

When one seeks to raise his own business apart from others, he tends to fail. On the other hand, when one seeks to raise the entire industry in which his business thrives, he tends to succeed—in his own business and as part of the greater whole. This has been especially true as our company has grown and expanded into foreign markets.

I called an old friend from Texas, Karl Rove, who happened to be the president's senior advisor, to complain. Karl knew why I was calling, of course, the minute he heard I was on the line. The issue of chicken export had been of international concern for some time, and Karl knew I wanted him to put more pressure on Russia's President Vladimir Putin. It wasn't only for the benefit of Pilgrim's Pride, by the way, but for the benefit of all chicken producers who were engaged in international export. Karl came on the line and rather curtly announced, "Bo, I'm up to my eyeballs today working on international terrorism in Afghanistan, a war in Iraq, homeland security, the economy, and this chicken business!" It was nice to know that the leaders of our nation had their priorities in order on that day—at least from my perspective.

We are a global player in the poultry industry, and the world is a difficult business environment even in the best of times.

GIVING TO THE
CAUSES YOU BELIEVE IN

Through the years, I've become a financial partner in the political process as well as an organizational leader and activist. I believe every business executive is smart to do so, but with this added advice:

- Make sure what you fund is legal.
- Make sure the folks behind the bill, the fund, or the campaign are talented, professional, and morally solid.
- Make sure you believe in the cause.

One organization of which I am a member is the Dallas Entrepreneurial Political Action Committee (DALENPAC). It was founded in 1978 by Arthur Wessely, Louis Beecherl, Bob Pickens, Bill Pickens, Mack Rankin, Frank West, and Al Wiederkehr. Originally the group was called the Dallas Energy PAC, but the name was changed to reflect the more varied interests of its trustees and governors. Trustees give $1,000 to the PAC, and governors give $5,000. DALENPAC supports conservative, pro-business candidates for the U.S. House of Representatives and U.S. Senate with an emphasis on wildcat or long-shot races. The supporters of the PAC are men and women who have had successful business careers and are committed to keeping free enterprise, pro-growth principles in our government.

In October of 2004 I was honored as the seventh recipient of the

Governor William P. Clements Jr. Award, which is given by DALENPAC to honor men and women who have supported conservative principles with their time, efforts, and money. I was very pleased to receive the award, but I'm even more pleased to be a giver to DALENPAC. It stands for principles that I value highly.

CHICKENGATE

As much as I have tried to play by the political rules, I've also had my share of political gaffes. I haven't always used the best judgment, but even when I didn't, I tried to make the best of the situation.

For example, on July 4, 1989, I visited the Texas Senate to lobby for changes in the laws about workers' compensation. I handed out $10,000 political contribution checks to eight lawmakers who were considered to be swing voters on the issue—and I did this just two days before the vote on the bill. What I did was neither a bribe nor illegal, but the incident was considered questionable.

When somebody in the media asked me about it, I admitted I had made a "bonehead mistake." Well, officials of the Dallas-based Bonehead University decided I should receive the Bonehead of the Year award in 1990. I accepted! To have free publicity for being a bonehead when you are known for a *boneless* product was too good an opportunity to pass up. I may have been the only person to appreciate the humor and irony in that, but all in all, the opportunity to appear in the Pilgrim hat with Henrietta at a Lakewood Country Club banquet was a good one.

Whether in politics, in public appearances and promotions, or in advertising, I have found that things have a way of working out to your advantage if you have a good product, a clear message, a clean heart, and a good sense of humor.

If you have a good product, make it better.

Let the world know you have a great product and don't stop promoting it.

Build a reputation for innovation, quality, and a dose of fun in your promotions.

You'll probably be pleasantly surprised at the results.

★　★　★

We know that all things work together for good
to those who love God.
(Rom. 8:28 NKJV)

5

The Chicken Chili Caper— and Other Mouth-Watering Escapades

One of our company slogans is, "We're passionate about our food." So am I personally. I like to eat good food. I like to talk about good food. I even like to cook good food.

One of the great escapades of my life began when the organizers of the world's first indoor Celebrity Chili Cook-Off at Billy Bob's in Fort Worth dared me in a media interview with a dare no self-respecting chicken man could refuse. The organizer of the festival, Don Reynolds, challenged me—with a laugh—to enter the contest with *chicken* chili. At the time, chili made with chicken was virtually unknown. He then said, "You're chicken if you don't enter."

What could I do? I've never been one to back down on a dare. I accepted the challenge, but had no idea what it would lead to.

My public relations man at the time, Richard Brown, and I collaborated with our wives on the recipe and got it to the point where it tasted pretty good. We then each made and took about five gallons of our chicken chili to the cook-off along with small cups and plastic spoons to give everyone there a taste. We also took along printed recipes on a handout that had a store discount coupon for our new whole boneless chickens. We gave the recipes and coupons to those who liked what they ate at our booth. Richard and I figured that, at the minimum, we'd gain some customers for our boneless chicken as a result of the contest. We were really surprised when the hard-core Chili Appreciation Society International (CASI) chili aficionados gave our chicken chili third prize!

We decided to take our chicken chili recipe on the road, and we joined the chili cook-off circuit. In the months that followed, we chalked up more awards—and thousands of customers for our boneless chicken product.

I was also honored to be asked to judge the World's Championship Chili Cook-Off at Terlingua, Texas. After a few years, I decided to retire from my career in chili cook-offs.

Let me assure you, it was a pretty amazing feat to come up with gallons of chicken chili, set up the exhibits, and coordinate various interviews and public-speaking engagements with these events. I knew it was worth it all, however, when I got word that our chicken chili recipe was entered into the *Congressional Record* by Senator John Tower. Below is what Senator Tower had to say on that fateful day of March 26, 1984. (The spelling and punctuation are just as the item appeared in the *Congressional Record*, vol. 130, no. 48, part II.)

Mr. President, the many benefits to mind and body of good chili are beyond dispute. My own State of Texas has led the way in the development and perfection of that manna from Heaven, that culinary triumph, chili made with beef—and no beans.

Now, I am proud to advise my colleagues that Texas has created for the world yet another chili innovation, made with chicken.

My good friend, Bo Pilgrim, a national leader in the poultry industry who has developed an innovative method for processing whole boneless chicken, has agreed to share his recipe for chicken chili. I do not suggest that chicken chili will, or even could, replace traditional beef chili; but I do urge my colleagues to try this pleasing dish. It will provide culinary variety for those who enjoy good chili, and a delicious alternative to those who do not have the fortitude to appreciate multi-alarm Texas chili.

Mr. President, I ask that Bo Pilgrim's chicken chili recipe be printed in the RECORD.

The recipe follows (Errors made in the Congressional Record have been corrected.):

★ BO PILGRIM'S CHICKEN CHILI—
NO BONES ABOUT IT
"It's Mind-Boggling" (with 50 Percent Less Fat)

Ingredients:

1	medium onion, chopped (1½ cups)
2	cloves garlic chopped
¼	cup cooking oil
2	lbs Pilgrim's Pride Whole Boneless Chicken (coarse ground in kitchen meat processor)
1	8 oz. can tomato sauce
3	cups water
4	tablespoons chili powder
2	tablespoons flour
2	teaspoons salt
2	tablespoons ground cumin
1	teaspoon granulated sugar
½	teaspoon cayenne pepper
4	chicken bouillon cubes
1	teaspoon black pepper
2	teaspoons paprika

In kettle, sauté onion and garlic in oil until limp. Add ground Pilgrim Boneless Chicken and braise. Add water, bouillon cubes, and tomato sauce. Add remaining dry ingredients. Mix well, cover, and simmer 30 minutes covered and 30 minutes uncovered. Makes 8 servings of ⅔ cup each.

I'M NOT SHY ABOUT
SHARING MY FAVORITES

I like chicken. I really do. I eat a lot of it, and through the years, my wife, Patty, has come up with some recipes that I like to eat again and again. I never tire of them.

I realize that most executives who write books don't share their favorite recipes, but then, most executives who write books don't produce chicken. So, I'm taking the liberty of sharing with you several of my favorites. Try them. You'll like them. (I hope you buy some extra chicken this week—and especially I hope that you buy Pilgrim's Pride.)

★GRILLED MARINATED CHICKEN BREASTS

Ingredients:
4   boneless, skinless chicken breasts
1   lemon
     olive oil
     Cavender's Greek Seasoning

Place four boneless, skinless chicken breasts flat, in a single layer, in a shallow glass pan. Squeeze ½ to 1 whole lemon over the chicken.

Drizzle with a small amount of a good-quality olive oil.

Sprinkle generously, to taste, with Cavender's Greek Seasoning and place the dish, covered with plastic wrap, in the refrigerator. Allow to marinate for 1 hour, then turn the breasts and repeat with the lemon juice, olive oil, and *Cavender's*.

Grill quickly on high, for about 5 to 7 minutes per side, but be careful not to overcook. Grilling time will vary based on the size of the chicken breast.

Serve immediately.

I never get tired of chicken done this way. —Bo

You can do lots of things with marinated chicken. You can slice it up on a bed of lettuce and add some vine-ripened tomatoes on the side. You can put it in a baguette that has been cut in half, brushed with butter, and toasted—perhaps adding honey mustard and grilled vegetables. You can serve it with a variety of vegetables as a main dish—perhaps roasted red peppers, fresh spinach, and sautéed mushrooms. It even goes well in an Oriental-style salad with diced red peppers, sliced celery, mandarin oranges, chopped cashew nuts, sesame seeds, shredded coconut (toasted), and an Asian dressing.

★Chicken Bits

Ingredients:

8	boneless, skinless chicken breast halves
½	cup unseasoned fine dry bread crumbs
¼	cup grated Parmesan cheese
1	teaspoon salt
1	teaspoon dried leaf thyme
1	teaspoon dried leaf basil
½	cup butter, melted

Cut each chicken breast half into 6 to 8 nuggets, each about 1½-inch square. Combine the bread crumbs, cheese, salt, and herbs. Dip the chicken nuggets in melted butter and then in the crumb mixture. Place in a single layer on a foil-lined baking sheet. Bake at 400 degrees for 10 minutes.

Yield will be 8 main-dish servings of 6 to 8 dozen nuggets each, or 16 appetizer servings.

These are great! —Bo

★ TURKEY BURGERS

Start with frozen preformed turkey burger patties.

For each turkey burger patty (4 oz.) use 1 tablespoon olive oil.

In an iron skillet, set the burner halfway between medium and low (on a gas range). Use low heat on an electric range. Do not thaw the burger. Cook the burger for 5 minutes on each side in the olive oil. Add a tablespoon of water and Cavender's Greek Seasoning on each side as the burger is turned. Total cooking time—5 minutes per side—is 10 minutes.

Try this with two eggs at breakfast!
Or have it as a burger at lunch or as an entrée at dinner. —Bo

★ CHICKEN SPAGHETTI

Ingredients:
2   large, whole chickens
    Water, enough to cover the chickens
1   large, sliced onion
2   bay leaves
2–4 stalks of celery
    Lots of black pepper
5   generous tablespoons chicken bouillon granules

Place all the ingredients in a large stock pot and bring to a boil. Turn down the temperature low enough to keep the chickens simmering for about 1 hour, or a little longer. The chickens should be cooked to a falling-off-the-bone tenderness.

Remove the chickens from the stock and allow to cool slightly. Remove the meat from the bones and chop to the desired-size pieces for your recipe. Dispose of the bones and skin, and strain the remaining stock. Set aside the stock. (The broth is much better than canned and freezes well. It does not require any additional salt because of the bouillon granules.) This is the method we always use for any recipe that calls for cooked chicken.

2	large chickens, prepared as above and chopped
4	cups chopped onion
4	cups chopped celery
	Chopped fresh garlic to taste
4	cups chopped green and red peppers
2	lbs. shredded cheddar cheese for topping
2	cans undiluted cream of mushroom soup
4	one-pound boxes of spaghetti (either long or elbow style), partially cooked and drained
1	small can tomato paste
2	cups tomato juice
	Salt and pepper to taste
	Ground Cumin to taste, usually a generous amount
2	small bottles Mexene chili powder, or to taste
1	large can sliced mushrooms
	Reserved chicken stock
	Shredded Cheddar for topping

Sauté the onion, celery, garlic, and peppers until tender. In a large pan combine all the ingredients, except the cooked chicken and the cheese for topping. Add enough of the reserved chicken stock from the above recipe to make the mixture very moist. Simmer gently on the stove top for about 15 to 20 minutes, adding more stock as needed and stirring occasionally to prevent scorching. Add the chopped, cooked chicken and turn mixture into one large, or several smaller, oven-proof casserole dishes. Top with the remaining cheddar cheese. This dish can be refrigerated or frozen until ready to use and is a nice make-ahead dish for busy times.

Bake at 350° oven until heated through and bubbly and nicely browned. Serve immediately. It satisfies a large crowd of hungry eaters.

I could eat this for two hours straight. —Bo

★CHICKEN SALAD

Ingredients:
    cooked, cubed chicken breast meat
    mayonnaise
    chopped celery
    salt and pepper

Mix ingredients to the consistency and seasoning desired. Great on lettuce or bread.

I have this several times a week. —Bo

★ ★ ★

Freely you have received,
freely give.
(Matt. 10:8 NKJV)

6

TRYING TO STAY OUT
OF SOME HEADLINES

As much as I have enjoyed the limelight and fun of doing commercials and promotional events, there are other times when I wish Pilgrim's Pride could have stayed *out* of the headlines. Most people who have been in business for any length of time know that not all publicity is good publicity.

Amateur boxing was very popular in my part of the world when I was a young man. Some of the fights were spontaneous—the "side show" of a country dance. It seemed young men and women who gathered from different small communities were a little suspicious of one another. The young men, it seemed, were particularly protective and jealous of "their girls." When a guy from another community would try to date one of our girls in Pine, there was nearly always a commotion.

We also did a lot of "official" boxing in Pine. We had a boxing ring near the store, and kids as well as teenagers and adults would box. There was an adult boxing tournament in Pittsburg, and I recall my father telling about one particular trip he made to this tournament. A couple of guys were sitting near my father, and it seemed that just about every bout had someone announced as being "from Pine, Texas." One of these guys punched the other one and said, "They must be fighting sons of a gun in Pine." The other said, "I don't know about fighting, but those are the lyingest sons of a gun."

Fighters and liars! It wasn't much of a reputation for a man from Pine to have!

Throughout my life, I haven't minded fighting for causes I believe in—but not with my fists. I have totally rejected lying, however. I have wanted to be known as a person of integrity. I want our Partners to be people known for integrity in all of their dealings. I want the basis of my decision making to be this: do what is right. And I want our Partners to have that same philosophy as the basis of their decision making. For the most part, people know what is right.

"No lying" is what's right—even when dealing with what might be considered a sticky issue.

In the poultry business, there are five very important issues:

1. Biosecurity
2. Food safety
3. Employee safety
4. Animal welfare
5. Environmental stewardship

When I began in the chicken business, I had never heard the term *biosecurity*. Very few people—in fact, only those in academic research circles—seemed to use the word *environmental*. Animal welfare was never discussed. Safety was considered more of an individual concern than a government issue.

Times have changed.

These are issues in which a good record is paramount. These are issues in which no news is good news, but they are also issues in which statements do need to be made if bad news isn't accurate news.

1. THE CONCERNS ABOUT BIOSECURITY

Biosecurity is a major concern in all poultry companies. In the middle of the last century, diseases in chickens usually were isolated to a small farm.

Once a chicken got sick, there was very little a person could do for it. In fact, the only "experts" in the field when it came to chicken health were the people who were raising chickens. The county agents generally weren't poultry specialists. There were no antibiotics especially geared to poultry, much less inoculation of chickens.

As chicken houses got larger in the 1950s, it was easier for disease to spread from flock to flock, and both medications and new standards for preventing disease were developed. The antibiotics came in the 1950s, but as we all know, viruses mutate and new diseases always seem to be identified. In the late 1960s, for example, the chicken industry had a major problem with something called Marek's disease, which left the bird's skin malformed. The disease didn't make the food unsafe, but because of the abnormality, the government condemned chickens that acquired it. At one point, the industry was losing 10 to 15 percent of its product to Marek's. Then researchers developed a vaccine, and today, virtually anybody who is new to the industry has never heard of Marek's.

Another tool in controlling disease has been the spacing out of chicken houses. The farther apart chicken farms are spaced, the better the management practices.

Cleanliness, of course, is the best prevention tool of all.

A number of precautions are taken routinely. For example, employees who have come into contact with other poultry, wild birds, or pet birds may not be allowed to work in certain live production areas of the company.

A person who visits a large chicken producer these days may have to drive his vehicle through a tire wash. This procedure is particularly important for vehicles that visit more than one farm a day. An antibiotic wash ensures that pathogens that might be picked up on one farm will not be transmitted to another. Those who enter a chicken house often have to step through a foot wash that kills pathogens on the soles of shoes. Some chicken house operators insist that visitors wear hairnets, coveralls, and disinfected boots. Visitors are usually restricted to specific areas. Why? Nobody knows better than the grower about how devastating an outbreak of disease can be to his chicken house, to his chickens, and ultimately to his profitability.

Those who enter a chicken house often have to step through a foot wash that kills pathogens on the soles of shoes. Some chicken house operators insist that visitors wear hairnets, coveralls, and disinfected boots. Visitors are usually restricted to specific areas.

Diseases that have been eliminated in the United States, of course, can thrive in many nations around the world.

Headlines in 2004 let us know that avian flu—very specifically the H5N1 strain of avian influenza—is floating around in Asia. Three people died from it in August of 2004 in Vietnam, two of them young children. Earlier in 2004, twenty-three people died in Vietnam and Thailand, according to the World Health Organization. Those who died had been exposed to sick poultry. Outbreaks of the avian flu in poultry flocks have been reported in Thailand, Indonesia, and China, as well as Vietnam. A different strain of the avian flu—H5N2 virus—was reported at two ostrich farms in the Eastern Cape province of South Africa.

Headlines like these are frightening to the general public. And what frightens the general public frightens those of us who are in the poultry-producing business!

The facts are these: we are vigilant at *all* times when it comes to the biosecurity of our poultry—not just when there's a bird flu outbreak halfway around the world. We take the utmost precautions to keep disease from entering a flock, and if that should happen, we take extreme measures to keep the disease from spreading.

Avian flu is *not* acquired by eating or handling processed poultry products. It has been acquired only rarely by human beings who have had close contact with infected live birds. Avian flu does not survive the cooking process for chicken.

2. FOOD SAFETY CASES ARE VERY RARE

Food contamination is rarely at the processing plant level. The statistics bear that out. Contamination nearly always occurs at the hands of the private consumer. Occasionally bad handling can happen in a store or restaurant.

People have told our customer service representatives that our chicken was bad by the time they got it to their dinner table. They want their money back, and we give them their moncy back—regardless of the reason for their dissatisfaction.

Invariably, however, when these people are questioned more closely about how they handled the products they had picked up at the store, we learn that they left the chicken in the trunk of the car under a hot sun for prolonged hours before they got the chicken home from the supermarket and into their own kitchens . . . or they left the chicken out to defrost in a hot pantry for several days before cooking it . . . or they failed to cook the chicken thoroughly (at least to 160 degrees for boneless chicken breast) . . . or they failed to wash their hands thoroughly as they prepared the chicken for cooking . . . or they failed to properly refrigerate the chicken leftovers after cooking.

Some contamination also occurs because people use utensils and cooking equipment in preparing salads and raw vegetables immediately after they've used those same utensils and bowls to cut up or prepare raw chicken. Any utensil or piece of equipment used in the handling of raw poultry should always be washed thoroughly with hot soapy water before it is used again for another purpose in the kitchen.

Chicken is a perishable product. It needs to be handled and stored properly.

3. PLANT SAFETY IS A TOP PRIORITY

One of the things I've been very concerned about from the very beginning of Pilgrim's Pride has been our corporate safety standards. People can't work and support their families if they are injured. If people are absent from work, not only does productivity suffer, but morale is dampened. A good safety record is a very high priority to me.

The government agency that oversees worker safety—Occupational Safety and Health Administration (OSHA)—establishes minimum safety standards to help protect people. Accidents can happen, of course. Nevertheless, we do our utmost to keep them from happening again because we believe that all accidents are preventable. I'm very pleased with our safety record, but I am devastated from time to time when an employee is injured, for whatever reason.

The industry average for the lost workday incident rate is 0.8. At Pilgrim's Pride, our current rate is 0.5—almost 40 percent better than the industry average.

A universally accepted measurement of safety performance is OSHA's lost workday incident rate. The industry average for the lost workday incident rate is 0.8. At Pilgrim's Pride, our current rate is 0.5—almost 40 percent better than the industry average.

We first began to receive outstanding honors for our safety records in 1993 when our Lufkin processing plant completed 3.5 million safe work hours without experiencing a lost-time injury. This set a national record for the poultry industry, and we were given the prestigious Award of Honor from the National Safety Council and letters of commendation from then Texas Governor Ann Richards and President Bill Clinton. In 1995 the same plant reached a new record of 3.6 million safe work hours without a lost-time injury. Keep in mind that these hours worked safely relate to facilities that have lots of moving pieces of machinery, and some use of knives!

We have achieved numerous other outstanding safety accomplishments, including:

- Nacogdoches, Texas, Hatchery and Live Haul have posted more than 12 years without a lost workday injury.
- Nacogdoches, Texas, Feed Mill posted more than 11 years without a lost workday injury.
- De Queen, Arkansas, Hatchery posted more than 10 years without a lost workday injury.
- Our processing plant in Marshville, North Carolina, reached 2 million safe work hours without a lost workday injury.
- Our processing plant in Enterprise, Alabama, reached 2 million safe work hours without a lost workday injury.
- Our Prepared Foods Plant in Canton, Georgia, reached 2 million safe work hours without a lost workday injury.
- Our processing plant in De Queen, Arkansas, reached 2 million safe work hours without a lost workday injury.
- Our El Dorado, Arkansas, processing plant was recognized by the Arkansas State Department of Labor after it had compiled 3 million safe work hours of operation without a lost-time accident. That plant has now topped 4 million hours without a lost-time accident.

Why am I telling you this?

Because what a company does about safety sends a very strong message about the way corporate leaders value their employees. A company that goes beyond minimum safety standards is a company that essentially says to its workers: "We want you well, we want you whole, we want you here on the job doing your best, and we want you to be everything you can be and to do the best you can do."

People are proud of safety records. A good record is a mark of achievement that has nothing to do with paychecks. It's a reflection of quality in processes and procedures. In most cases, employees who are aware of their accomplishment in posting good safety records become very competitive about them. They encourage one another to beat their own record—forming something of a companywide team that takes on the statistics as the foe rather than another company. To me, that's healthy competition.

If we're going to go for a knockout punch at Pilgrim's Pride, I want that to be a knockout punch against an old safety record. No blood, no pain . . . only glory.

A QUICKER REBUILDING

I have discovered through the years that people who are proud of their safety record, and who have high morale, are quicker to rebound from an accident or fire than those who have a poor safety record and low morale.

All manufacturing and processing plants face the possibility of mechanical failures regardless of the precautions taken. We had an incident in January 1992 when a fire erupted at our Prepared Foods plant in Mount Pleasant. A defective hydraulic line on a fry cooker came loose.

About a third of our local Partners were working in the plant when the fire broke out—1,100 people of the 3,200 employed. We successfully evacuated the facility, and only 4 people had to be admitted to the hospital—only one was seriously injured. The evacuation took less than five minutes, and the plant's own fire-surpression system extinguished the blaze by the time firefighters arrived. If we had pursued anything less than the maximum safety standards, we might have had a real tragedy. As it was, the blaze was contained to just one production line, and we were able to reopen in five days.

We also had a fire at our Lufkin, Texas, plant on July 25, 1993. The good news was that no one was injured. The bad news was that a significant portion of the plant was destroyed beyond repair. The *amazing* news was that the destroyed portion of the plant was rebuilt in seventy-eight days, which was a record for rebuilding a chicken processing facility. Our Partners really pulled together as a team, pooling equipment, ideas, and manpower. We didn't miss a single scheduled delivery to our regular customers.

The rebuilding effort required hauling 600 truckloads of debris from the site, as well as acquiring new equipment and building supplies. The new portion of the plant has 28,000 square feet, including 9.9 miles of cable, 63.96 miles of wire, and 217 new pieces of operating equipment. The plant at that time employed more than 700 people and was capable of processing 850,000 birds a week.

4. THE HUMANE TREATMENT OF ANIMALS IS A *MUST*

I believe in the humane treatment of animals, but I also believe God has provided us with chickens and other animals for food and nourishment. Genesis 9:1–4 spells it out plainly:

> Be fruitful and multiply, and fill the earth . . . Every beast of the earth . . . every bird of the air . . . all that move on the earth . . . all the fish of the sea . . . they are given into your hand. Every moving thing that lives shall be food for you. I have given you all things, even as the green herbs. But you shall not eat flesh with its life, that is, its blood.

People can choose to be vegetarians if they want, but God certainly has never commanded His people to be vegetarians. Later in the Bible we find lists of foods that God considered "unclean" for His people to eat—for their health's sake. Chicken is *not* on that list!

In order for people to eat chicken, the chickens have to be processed. They should be processed humanely and efficiently, in a way that results in as little trauma to the chicken as possible.

I certainly respect the right of animal activist groups to promote a vegetarian lifestyle, but I do *not* believe any group has the right to lie or misrepresent facts, cause physical harm to employees or property of organizations with which they disagree, or push their agenda on others.

Let me address very briefly the issue of media coverage for animal activist groups. In my opinion, these groups are often given far more serious coverage than they deserve simply because they tend to be loud and disruptive in their demonstrations and outlandish in their claims. People need to be very careful in repeating these groups' claims without first verifying whether or not they are true. When something is reported that turns out to be false, equal space needs to be given to admitting the error and presenting the truth. People also need to dig a little deeper at times and find out just how many people are protesting, and for what reasons.

In July 2004, we were made aware of a videotape showing mistreatment and mishandling of live birds at one of our chicken processing plants in Moorefield, West Virginia. We were appalled at the treatment of the animals shown in this video. The actions were completely contrary to all of our company's practices and policies regarding the humane treatment of poultry, and were not in any way condoned by management.

We immediately launched an aggressive and thorough investigation. The next day, we suspended one employee without pay and began investigating three others. We made it clear that any employees who were found to have violated our policies on animal welfare would be terminated.

We temporarily stopped production at all twenty-five processing plants to review our animal-welfare policies with *every* employee and supervisor who handles live animals, and we required signatures from each of these employees to reaffirm their understanding of the policies.

One day later, we fired eleven employees, including one superintendent, one supervisor, one foreman, and eight hourly employees, for violating our animal-welfare policies at the Moorefield facility.

We engaged Dr. Temple Grandin, one of the world's foremost experts in the field of animal welfare, to review the Moorefield plant's animal welfare practices.

I was also very troubled to hear that the person who supposedly witnessed these abuses—a so-called "animal welfare investigator"—did not immediately report them to *us*. Although he worked at our plant for more than eight months—and had signed our animal welfare policy promising to report any animal abuses to management immediately—no abuses were reported until the day before he quit, when an anonymous report was made to our hotline. And the videotaped evidence was not made available to Pilgrim's Pride management for two more months. Had he presented the videotaped evidence earlier or told us about his discoveries, we could have taken corrective and disciplinary actions much earlier.

I will not tolerate any mistreatment of our animals by any of our employees. Any employee who mistreats animals in violation of company policy is terminated immediately.

Let me say for the record that I will not tolerate any mistreatment of our animals by any of our employees. Any employee who mistreats animals in violation of company policy will be terminated immediately. In fact, under the terms of Pilgrim's Pride employment, any employee who observes violations of the company's animal-welfare policies is obligated to report them immediately to his or her supervisor.

From a management standpoint, I recognize that as much as any company tries to hire excellent people, treat them in an excellent way, and entrust them with important responsibilities, no management team can fully ensure that some employees will not break corporate policies and rules willfully and maliciously.

Animal welfare is a serious matter. Not only because treating our birds well is the right thing to do, but because good treatment of the chickens helps assure high-quality, healthful products.

5. FARMERS ARE THE FOREMOST ENVIRONMENTALISTS I KNOW

Every good farmer I know is an environmentalist at heart. Good steward-ship of the earth, air, and water is basic to good farming. No one cares more about the quality of the water and soil than the farm families who live where they work. Many of our growers' farms have been in the family for generations, and these farmers intend to pass them on to their children for generations to come.

Good environmental practices are vital to me on two main fronts. First, as a Christian, I consider it a sacred duty to be a good steward of this earth that God created and entrusted to us human beings for care. I cannot expect God's best from His earth if I am not willing to do my best for His earth—including the land, water, and air.

Second, in the long run, good environmental practices are good business. The renewable resources of this earth produce more if they are routinely replenished, restored, and enriched.

In most parts of the country, the by-products of chicken farming are considered tremendous assets that fertilize pastures for the grazing of cattle and the sides of highways for a beautiful landscape.

In 1987 we created a dewatering press to remove solid particles from waste water. This division of the company lost money for several years so we finally sold it to Andritz-Ruthner, Inc., which had previous experience in this type of business. The firm runs the operation successfully, and to our benefit, Andritz-Ruthner is located near our feed mill on South Texas Street in Pittsburg.

The main concern for many people has been whether chicken waste is finding its way into municipal water supplies. At Pilgrim's Pride we have spent thousands of hours and untold amounts of money to produce systems of pasture irrigation that keep biosolids from chicken houses out of water sources by applying them to pastures at agronomic rates as a form of fertilizer. As far as I'm concerned, this is an outstanding means of reusing and recycling—one part of a farm benefits another part of the farm, and the entire process remains organic.

In addition, our contract growers' poultry houses are specially designed to prevent contamination of groundwater supplies and soil erosion, and Pilgrim's Pride growers are encouraged to use best management practices, including litter storage and composting facilities, where appropriate. We emphasize proper handling and management of litter and flock mortality, and we require compliance with all state and local environmental laws and regulations.

Along with our growers and Partners, Pilgrim's Pride proudly accepts our responsibility as a steward of the land, air, and water. We invest in modern agricultural practices and commit talent, time, research and resources to protect the environment as a part of our day-to-day activities.

I am very proud that Pilgrim's Pride Corporation and many of our growers have earned awards in recognition of our environmental stewardship.

What the Consumer Wants— and Wants to Know

Through the years, I have come to believe that what the consumer wants is a safe, high-quality product in the supermarket or at the fast-food outlet or restaurant, and that's what we aim to supply. Consumers trust that the companies that produce their food care about food safety, employee safety and health, environmental stewardship, animal welfare, and other important issues. Of course, all companies have their challenges from time to time, and sometimes these issues are sensationalized in the media. Unfortunately, a great deal of harm can be done to a company that has an overall outstanding record but is falsely accused or maligned by slanted or inaccurate reporting.

What *is* good is when mistakes in these areas come to light within a company—when problems are brought to the attention of the people who can fix them.

No executives I know in the food industry—or any industry for that matter—intentionally seek to harm their customers. The exact opposite is true. What I don't understand is why some people in the media seem to willfully seek to harm responsible companies that routinely produce good products for the economic benefit of their own communities.

At Pilgrim's Pride we take care of our people, we take care of our birds, we take care of the food we process and prepare, and we take care of the environment. It's the right thing to do, and it's good business, too.

★ ★ ★

Whatever you do, do all to the
glory of God.
(1 Cor. 10:31 NKJV)

7

A Winning Strategy
and Partners Who Are Winners

Texans don't like to lose, and I'm a Texan.

We like to win in football . . . in beauty pageants . . . in politics . . . in acreage of ranches . . . and in the poultry business! Winning takes persistence—an ongoing commitment to goals and values.

One of our top executives once said that I'm "half pit bull." I don't mind that description in the least. I certainly am not a vicious man, but I know that isn't what this man meant. He meant that when I sink my teeth—my mind, my heart, my commitment—into something, I don't let go. He also said, "There's no give-up in Bo."

If I give you my word, I stick with what I said.

If I'm loyal to you today, you can count on my being loyal to you tomorrow.

If I make a commitment, I keep that commitment.

If I start a project, I finish it.

What I am, I hope others around me also are.

Persistence, as valuable a trait as it is, isn't enough. Winning takes more than raw courage and guts. To win, a team needs a game plan. Every small-town high school coach in Texas knows the value of having a winning strategy—and so do I.

The specifics for our strategies, of course, are trade secrets—just like the winning plays of a football coach. Nevertheless, I'm happy here to give you some insights into our company by sharing the statements that guide us. We found it of great advantage to put our business mission and strategy into focus on just one page of paper so that any person—customer, vendor, Partner, manager, or investor—could read it quickly.

Our Purpose: Within God's will, to help save rural North America and the family farms in the United States, Puerto Rico, and Mexico, by the creation of jobs through the production of healthy and economical chicken, turkey, and egg products for the rest of the world. It is our commitment to seek to protect and enhance God's environmental resources through the use of the best affordable and practical science, technology, and animal welfare practices available for use in the agriculture industry. By applying these industry best management practices to our uses of the land, water, and air resources, we will operate within local, state and federal rules and regulations and demonstrate our commitment toward environmental stewardship. We will always give God the credit for our progress in, or achievement of, this purpose.

Our Mission Statement: Our job is outstanding customer satisfaction . . . every day.

We guarantee that if a customer is not satisfied with the quality of our product, he can send proof of purchase and price for a full refund.

Vision: To be a world-class food company . . . better than the best.

To me, being world-class means having financial strength, facilities, management expertise, and motivated Partners who can compete and *win* against competitors anywhere in the world.

Core Values: At Pilgrim's Pride, our core values are our foundation. Our values guide us in our daily decisions and dictate our overall business strategy.

We will strive to be a company of people **known for integrity** in all of our dealings. The basis of our decisions will be *doing what is right*, not just in terms of that which is technically correct, but by doing that which is just, fair, and equitable in light of the circumstances. We will deal **honestly and non-deceptively** with our word as our bond, and expect reciprocity; living up to the spirit, not just the letter, of the law.

To these statements, which are basic statements made by many companies, we add a statement that isn't often made—a statement of guiding principle. It is the foundation for all other statements.

Our Guiding Principle: The Golden Rule: However you want people to treat you, so treat them (Matt. 7:12).

You'll find our guiding principle on the first page, as the first statement in our Partner Handbook. Our mission and guarantee flow from that guiding principle, and I have no doubt that if we stay committed to this guiding principle, we will fulfill our vision to be better than the best on the world stage.

We state several other things right up front in this handbook that you may find interesting. I'm a firm believer in first things first, and these statements on the first two pages of this handbook set the tone for how we do things at Pilgrim's Pride. They are *not* just words. They are a reflection of the way I choose to live my personal life, and how I want our Partners to conduct themselves.

Strategic Objectives:
- Be the preferred supplier to our customers.
- Grow at twice the industry rate.
- Be in the top 25 percent in efficiencies in all processes and services.
- Consistently earn a net profit of 4 percent or more to create value for our shareholders.
- Be a great place to work!

Management Philosophy: Continuous Improvement.

Our Partners: We acknowledge our Partners as our most valued asset, respecting them, providing fair compensation, meaningful work, fair treatment, and a safe work environment. *Continuous Improvement* will be our guiding management philosophy. Recognizing the potential within each person, we will empower Partners with authority at the lowest level reasonably possible.

We will require accountability both for results and for the methods by which they are accomplished.

Partners are expected to be loyal and fully dedicated to their jobs; however, we acknowledge the importance of each Partner's personal life and recognize the need to balance one's work with spiritual needs, family needs, and personal needs.

A GOOD PARTNER

1. Is known for integrity in all of his or her dealings.
2. Does what is just, fair, and equitable in light of the circumstances.
3. Is honest.
4. Lives up to the spirit—not just the letter—of the law.
5. Participates in Continuous Improvement in improved designs, reduced cost, improved quality and services to our customers.
6. Recognizes the potential within each person.
7. Is loyal.
8. Is fully dedicated to his or her job.
9. Balances his or her personal life with work, health, family, and spiritual needs.

I have been very blessed to have an outstanding senior management team. Their leadership experience totals more than three hundred years in the poultry business! We have a solid core of middle management, which positions the company very well for future growth and development. Our real hidden strength lies in our more than 40,000 dedicated Partners and 5,000 contract growers.

HALLMARKS OF A WINNING PARTNER

I may not know a lot about what it takes to create a winning recipe in the kitchen—through the years, I have left that to the experts, and mainly to my wife, Patty. However, I do know what has been our winning recipe in business:

- Use the best ingredients.
- Handle the ingredients with care—with thorough, painstaking review and due diligence.
- Prepare with skill, using dedicated and well-trained teams working through every detail.
- Serve with pride.

I believe the first three of these recipe factors also relate to winning Partners. We seek to hire the best people, handle them with care, and prepare them for their jobs with sufficient training in every detail. We know that they will have pride in what they do if we do our part.

Most businesspeople have a certain amount of skill at evaluating a business opportunity. Some are more trained than others. Some just seem to have an uncanny ability to sense a good deal. Equally important, I believe, is the ability to evaluate people, especially those who are seeking to work with you.

I look for a person who displays the following qualities.

GENUINE

I look for a person who is genuine. I like people who don't put on airs, who say what they mean, who have a sense of humor, and who are consistent from place to place, time to time, and situation to situation. What they believe, they say. What they say, they mean. When they say they are going to do something, they do it. They are who they are, through and through.

EAGER TO WORK

E. Stanley Jones was a great spiritual leader and adventurer around the world. He told this story:

> I once came down from Almore over one of the worst winding roads of the world. The driver of the bus had never driven in the Himalayas before, and it happened that on his first trip the previous day he had almost gone over one of those terrifying, precipitous cliffs. He was nervous; so before starting back he came in front of the engine and stood with folded hands, saying his prayers to the machine. That done, we started off, but had not gone far when the engine began to overheat. There was no water in the radiator! This was remedied. But when we were still many miles from our destination, the machine stopped while going up hill. There was no petrol in the tank! There we stayed until rescued. The driver said his prayers to the machine, but put no water in the radiator and no petrol in the tank. (found in William H. Danforth, *I Dare You!*, St. Louis, MO: American Youth Foundation, 1991, 88–89)

I believe very strongly in a faith that goes on the offensive by *doing something* practical and tangible. I like people who keep themselves busy doing something beneficial or positive. Once, I became very frustrated that an equipment failure had shut down our rendering plant in Mount Pleasant. I couldn't tolerate seeing some of my top men just standing around while technicians tried to sort out the problem so it could be repaired . . . so I handed all of them brooms. I wanted something to be done, even if it was cleaning the floor.

I always encourage those who do the hiring at Pilgrim's Pride to look for a person who is willing to work hard and to work until a job is finished.

My younger sister, Margaret, who I love dearly, worked with Aubrey and me for a number of years as the secretary at the feed mill. One day I caught her at the door, just waiting for the five o'clock whistle to blow. Her purse was in her hand—she was ready to walk out the moment that whistle sounded. I said to her, "Margaret, don't leave until the job is done." I never caught her standing at the door again.

I have a personal habit of getting up early so I can get a head start on the day. But my going-home policy has always been, "Don't leave until the jobs that need to be done that day are completed."

How can you know what needs to be done in a given day?

Once, I became very frustrated that an equipment failure had shut down our rendering plant in Mount Pleasant. I couldn't tolerate seeing some of my top men just standing around while technicians tried to sort out the problem so it could be repaired . . . so I handed all of them brooms. I wanted something to be done, even if it was cleaning the floor.

I don't know of any formula for that, but I do know that just about every manager I've ever met has a good understanding on any given day what *must* be accomplished in that day for the job to be done in a satisfactory way.

Those who leave work with a job left undone often experience far more stress than those who stay a little longer and complete the work. Those who finish a job are also a lot more eager to get to work the next day—a "left-undone" job becomes a "leftover" job, and most people don't find it motivating to have to face leftovers early in the morning.

A person eager and willing to work until the job is done is likely to be faithful and loyal, which are also traits I greatly admire in a Partner.

FAITHFUL AND LOYAL

You can't buy or train loyalty and faithfulness. It's not a matter of intelligence or education. We have a Partner that everyone knows in our organization. His name is Bill, and he is not a highly educated man. I'm not sure he can read. But this man is a dedicated worker. He mows the lawn around our buildings, and he gets rid of the weeds. He is a faithful and loyal employee. He openly talks about his preacher and his relationship with Lord Jesus. I consider him highly valuable.

Rayfield Bennett is another man who has been extremely loyal and faithful to me. He worked with my older brother Harold on his farm when he was just a boy, and later, he worked for Aubrey and me. He was with the retail feed store and warehouse for fifteen years, and then transferred to the feed mill where he's been working for approximately forty years. That's a long time for an employee to stick with you. I'm grateful.

LEARNING AND GROWING

One of the best traits in an employee is the ability to admit a mistake, learn from it, and never make it again. The difficulty with this trait is that you often don't discover it until a person makes a mistake and needs your forgiveness!

Years ago my son Ken came to me upset that a man seemed to be stealing from the company. He wanted to fire the man. I said, "Ken, sit down with this man. Give him an opportunity to admit his wrongdoing. If he does admit what you suspect he has done, say to him, 'If you do this again, you'll be firing yourself from this company.' If the man changes, you'll have an honest and more loyal employee. You'll be ahead in the long run. If you fire the man, you might find that you've hired a replacement person who also steals."

Through the years, I've taken this approach with several of our mid-level managers. In each case, there was very strong evidence of wrongdoing. Two of the men admitted their faults, were grateful for a second chance, and became long-standing, excellent employees. Two didn't admit their faults, and very soon after, they left of their own volition because they feared their wrongdoing would be revealed in even greater ways.

Why take an approach of forgiveness and a second chance? Because everybody makes mistakes. Everybody needs forgiveness. Everybody needs mercy.

Certainly I don't advocate allowing somebody to continue a pattern of wrongdoing, but in most cases, if you can help an employee change his or her ways and grow in character, he or she will be a good employee from that point on. You'll have saved yourself the expenses associated with firing the person and then hiring and training somebody new. It usually takes far less time and money to train and then retrain an employee—or to discipline and keep an employee—than to hire a new employee.

The truth is, sometimes the very person or situation that might seem to be a liability turns out to be a tremendous asset.

We had something of a humorous lesson in this many years ago as Patty and I made plans to go to the Cotton Bowl. We invited one of my childhood friends and first employees, James Shaddix, and his wife to go with us. James had broken his leg a few months earlier, and he was afraid he'd be a liability on the trip. I insisted that he go. When we arrived at the game, I said to the parking attendant, "I have a man on crutches," and we were given a priority parking space as close to the gate as possible. James wasn't in the least a hindrance—he was an asset!

The people you sometimes have a little trouble with at the outset of their employment can often be challenged and trained to be among your best workers over the years. Don't give up on people too soon.

THE SUPREME IMPORTANCE OF GOOD CHARACTER

There's one factor that rises above all those I've mentioned thus far. It's the factor of character. It's at the base of what makes a person genuine.

It's what motivates a person to work hard, be faithful and loyal, and learn and grow through mistakes.

One of my friends paid me a tremendous compliment recently. He told a mutual friend, "If I needed Bo, he'd be here in a minute. He's the first person outside my family that I'd call in an emergency."

That's the type of person I want to have working alongside me.

There are several things that I am convinced God wants every person to be. He sets the standards—we don't. God especially challenges Christians to be:

- *Loving* (1 Sam. 18:1–4; 19:1–7; 20:4–42). Jesus challenges us to love others regardless of their actions or responses to us.
- *Joyful* (Ps. 16:11; John 15:10–11; Rom 15:13). Christian joy comes from the Lord, not from outward circumstances.
- *Peaceable* (Gen. 26:17–31). True peace is a positive relationship first with the Lord, next with ourselves, and then with others.
- *Persevering* (1 Sam. 1:1–7, 10–17, 19–20). The Lord enables believers to persevere in the midst of difficulties and not lose heart.
- *Kind* (2 Kings 4:1–17). God desires that we treat people as individuals of worth, doing acts of goodness on their behalf, expecting nothing in return.
- *Right acting* (2 Kings 22:1–13, 18–20; 23:21–25). Doing right is a result of a right relationship with God.
- *Faithful* (Gen. 6:5–9, 12–14, 22; 7:1–3, 5; 8:1; Heb. 11:7). Being faithful is obeying what God says.
- *Humble* (Ex. 18:14–24; Num. 12:3; Heb. 11:24–26). Being humble is using your power and strength in doing loving and great things for others.
- *Under Control* (Dan. 1:1–15). God gives believers the power to be self-controlled. Those who discipline themselves when they are young are able to live their entire lives for the Lord.

I have taught these principles to my Sunday School class. I believe they are in the form of commandments to Christians, and they certainly are things I seek to reflect in my own life. I have absolutely no doubt that God promises to help Christians reflect these character traits in their lives if they desire to do so.

As chairman of the board, I cannot require that any board member, member of the executive team, or Partner pursue these character qualities. There are three things, however, that I *can* do.

First, I can make every effort possible to reflect these qualities in my life and in my interactions with others—including interactions on the job and in the community.

Second, I can openly encourage others to choose with their individual will to make the development of good character a priority in their personal lives. I can encourage our Partners to display the behaviors that flow from the character traits just noted. I can challenge them to be:

- Caring and generous in showing appreciation, which is the most appropriate expression of love in the workplace.
- Positive in their attitude, speech, and behavior, which is an expression of joy.
- Peace-seeking—attempting to resolve any conflict before it escalates or turns to bitterness.
- Patient and persistent—believing that each person can and will manifest his best side, and that every problem will eventually be resolved in a beneficial manner.
- Kind—treating others as people of worth and doing good deeds on their behalf without expecting something in return.
- Truthful, honest, and moral in their relationships with other Partners.
- Faithful to doing the best job possible, being diligent in putting in a full day's work for a full day's pay, and keeping the spirit of the regulations within the company to the best of their ability.

- Humble—a trait that is desirable in all people, but increasingly important, I believe, the higher the person is on the organizational chart.
- Under control—to take responsibility for their own actions and decisions.

Some people who are reading through this list are likely to conclude, "That's just plain ol' good behavior," or "That's the way all people should act toward one another in a civilized society." One woman said, "This is what it means to be a nice person." I couldn't agree more. If ever we needed workplaces with nice people as the prevailing norm, it's today. We face enough pressures in our fast-paced world of escalating information, continual deadlines, and long work shifts without having the added pressure of emotional and interpersonal tension filling our work spaces.

Through the years, I have encountered a number of work environments in which management and staff members did not reflect these character traits. There are countless work environments in which people are in a dog-eat-dog struggle for power and position. There are work environments in which there's a great deal of gossip, backstabbing, manipulation, and suspicion—you can feel the tension in the air just walking through some offices and factories.

I hope nobody who walks through our workplace at Pilgrim's Pride ever comes away feeling that way about us.

Third, I can encourage, applaud, and openly recognize and appreciate those who manifest these character traits toward me—or whom I see manifesting these traits toward others. I can motivate people to continue to display these character traits by acknowledging that I value their behavior and that I consider them to be good role models.

When it comes right down to it, I don't believe a corporation can be better than the composite character of all its people. Character traits can't help becoming evident in relationships with customers. They can't help being manifested in times when problems surface—such as a day when supplies are late, equipment breaks down, or quotas aren't met. Character traits are at the very heart of corporate morale.

The Value of Expressing High Goals and Emphasizing Character

I believe there is tremendous value in expressing a corporation's highest goals and purposes, and in placing an emphasis on character traits. People want to know what you stand for. They want to know who you are—and even if you fail at times, they want to know who you aspire to be.

Good people produce good. Who we are can't help coming out in what we do.

I'm excited about the depth of management in our company and the organization we have assembled to compete in the future. (See pages 100–103 for the names of our board of directors and senior management team.) Consolidation has given Pilgrim's Pride one of the best—or perhaps *the* best—"Team Management" organizations in our industry as a result of talent acquired from three major acquisitions we've made in recent years: Green Acre Foods, WLR Foods, and ConAgra's chicken division. Combining this new talent with Pilgrim's Pride leadership has helped us ensure our future competitiveness. These are all very good people, both personally and professionally.

At the same time, goodness is not something a person can dictate. It's only something a leader at the top can model for those with whom he or she works. Character is something I value and work at every day of my life. The mission statements, goals, and statements of integrity are things I personally believe in and aspire to achieve. The guiding principle of Pilgrim's Pride is my personal guiding principle. No executive has the right or authority to tell another person how to live if he isn't personally willing to live that way.

PILGRIM'S PRIDE
BOARD OF DIRECTORS

From left to right: LONNIE KEN PILGRIM, Executive Vice President, Assistant to Chairman; RICHARD A. COGDILL, Executive Vice President, Chief Financial Officer, Secretary and Treasurer; LONNIE "BO" PILGRIM, Chairman; O. B. GOOLSBY, JR., President and Chief Executive Officer; CLIFFORD E. BUTLER, Vice Chairman

From left to right: JAMES G. VETTER, JR., Attorney, Godwin, White and Gruber, PC, Professional Corporation, Dallas, Texas; DONALD L. WASS, PH.D., President, The William Oncken Company of Texas, Dallas, Texas; LINDA CHAVEZ, President, Center for Equal Opportunity, Sterling, Virginia; VANCE C. MILLER, SR., Chairman of Vance C. Miller Interests, Chairman and Chief Executive Officer of Henry S. Miller Cos., Dallas, Texas

From left to right: S. KEY COKER, Executive Vice President, Compass Bank, Dallas, Texas; KEITH W. HUGHES, Consultant and former CEO of Associates First Capital, Dallas, Texas; CHARLES L. BLACK, Retired Banker, Mount Pleasant, Texas; BLAKE D. LOVETTE, Retired Poultry Executive, North Wilkesboro, North Carolina

PILGRIM'S PRIDE
CORPORATION

OFFICERS

Lonnie "Bo" Pilgrim, Chairman

Clifford E. Butler, Vice Chairman

O.B. Goolsby, Jr., President and Chief Executive Officer

Richard A. Cogdill, Executive Vice President,
Chief Financial Officer, Secretary and Treasurer

J. Clinton Rivers, Chief Operating Officer

Robert A. Wright, Executive Vice President,
Sales and Marketing

EXECUTIVE VICE PRESIDENTS

Robert L. Hendrix, Executive Vice President,
Case Ready and Supply Operations

Lonnie Ken Pilgrim, Executive Vice President,
Assistant to Chairman

INTERNATIONAL OPERATIONS

Alejandro M. Mann, President, Mexico Operations

Hector L. Mattei-Calvo, President, Puerto Rico Operations

SENIOR VICE PRESIDENTS

Jane T. Brookshire, Senior Vice President,
Human Resources

William D. Bussell, Senior Vice President,
Supply Plants Regional Operations

Senior Vice Presidents (cont.)

Mark S. Chranowski, Senior Vice President,
Fresh Food Service and International Operations

John H. Curran, Senior Vice President,
Consumer Division

Joseph R. Gardner, Jr., Senior Vice President,
Case Ready Business Management

David W. Hand, Senior Vice President,
International and Fresh Sales

William V. Kantola, Senior Vice President,
Foodservice Sales

Michael D. Martin, Senior Vice President,
Case Ready Regional Operations

Joseph R. Menefee, Senior Vice President,
Prepared Foods Regional Operations

Joseph Moran, Senior Vice President,
Fresh Food Service, Regional Operations

Ronald E. Morris, Senior Vice President,
Turkey Sales and Operations

Robert N. Palm, Senior Vice President,
Case Ready Regional Operations

Michael A. Pruitt, Senior Vice President,
Live Production Technical Services

Walter F. Shafer, III, Senior Vice President,
Prepared Foods Regional Operations

Timothy G. Thomas, Senior Vice President,
Procurement

Senior Vice Presidents (cont.)

Gary L. Treat, Senior Vice President,
Food Safety and Quality Assurance

Gary D. Tucker, Senior Vice President,
Corporate Controller

James W. Tunnell, Jr., Senior Vice President,
Information Technology and Chief Information Officer

★ ★ ★

You will know them by their fruits . . . Every
good tree bears good fruit.
(Matt. 7:16–17 NKJV)

8

STIRRING UP THE
FIRES OF HIGH MORALE

Work defines our lives to a great extent; therefore, for an employee to be satisfied, work needs to have meaning and purpose.

One of the ways I try to instill meaning and purpose in our people is to call them by a name that I genuinely mean: Partners. The people who work with me are partners in two very real ways.

First, they are our partners in improving the quality of our products and processes. I look to our employees to tell me how to do things better and how to be of greater service to our customers.

Second, they are my partners in our efforts to feed the world. The needs for a healthy diet and high-quality protein are not just the needs of people in the United States; they are the needs of people around the world. All of us are in a great campaign—both an opportunity and a responsibility—to be part of the solution that feeds the world.

Partnership means that people are working together, and more specifically they are working together as team players. It is a human tendency to overestimate what we can do by ourselves and underestimate what we can do as a group. I'm all for team management. And I believe we can further enhance any team process by adding prayer and seeking the Lord's guidance.

I have mentioned Dr. James Miner previously as our primary nutritionist, but Dr. Miner was also our senior vice president of live production for many years. He joined us in 1966 and was a key figure in all phases of management at the company. He played a key role in the design and equipment selection for Hatchery No. 2, which was constructed as a state-of-the-art facility in 1988.

One of the foremost things I always appreciated about Dr. Miner was his willingness to be part of the larger team. If we were facing a problem, Dr. Miner would respond, "Tell me what you want me to do, and we'll do it." He never put his department or personal desires ahead of what was good for the whole company. If the company faced a crisis related to weather, growout and hatchery expansions, or problems with yield, contamination, or bruises, Dr. Miner was always willing to take more than his share of responsibility for correcting the problem. He did so in a professional and untiring manner. He worked hard solving nutrition, disease, and planning and scheduling problems in our Arkansas and Mexico expansions, just as he had in our Texas operations.

High morale in a company flows out of a partnership perspective—a perspective of people encouraging one another as players on the same team. At the core of morale, however, is the factor called "fire in the belly." It motivates a person to compete, to choose to be on a team, and to choose to give his or her best for the team.

FIRE IN THE BELLY

There's no substitute for a person having a very strong drive to make a contribution in this world—through business, volunteer efforts, or parenting. The focus of the drive isn't nearly as important as having the drive in the first place. Give me a person who has fire in his belly, and I can help that person find a purpose and focus for his driving ambition. Fire in the belly can be focused, used, directed, and made productive.

But how do you start a fire in someone who has no drive, no ambition, no deep desire to accomplish anything or to leave a mark in this world? It's a nearly impossible task in my opinion. I've worked with a lot of highly motivated people to help them discover their talents and channel their energies into projects and tasks that are very important and rewarding. I've never had any success in trying to motivate someone who would rather sit by the side of the road and watch the world go by.

Part of having fire in the belly means having an abiding hope that things can and will get better if you work hard enough, believe in the right things, and display the right character.

In many ways, fire in the belly is close to having a survival instinct. If you are going to survive, you must have two things:

A big dose of can-do spirit. That seemed to come to me naturally— maybe it was my family; maybe it was just being born and raised in Texas. I always thought I could succeed with God's help. I might not have been sure about the nature of that success or the path to that success in my earlier years, and I was never fully sure of the final magnitude of the success, but I was sure I could succeed.

My faith backs up that can-do spirit. The apostle Paul wrote to the Philippians: "I can do all things through Christ who strengthens me" (Phil. 4:13 NKJV).

Raw courage. Just believing you can do something doesn't mean that you will actually step out and start doing it. Those who have only a can-do spirit are prone to become big dreamers with very little to show for their lives. They have potential, but make no contribution to the world. It takes raw courage to say, "I can do this and I'm *going* to do this . . . now watch me try."

I have always had a Texas-sized dose of can-do spirit and courage.

Let me assure you of this, however: as much as I applaud and appreciate those who have fire in the belly, if I have to make a choice between a person with good character and fire in the belly, I'll take character. A person with fire in the belly and no character is a wildfire about to be set.

On the other hand, a person with good character who also has fire in the belly can set the world on fire in a positive way—he or she is going to rise to the highest levels of leadership.

STIRRING UP THE FIRE

There's a difference between trying to create fire in the belly in another person and stirring up fire. Sometimes a person will have latent or "unkindled" fire in the belly. It's a leader's role to identify that fire and stir it up.

William Danforth tells this story in his book, *I Dare You!*:

> Henry Woods, one of our promising boys, pushed through the door of my office early one morning and stood facing me defiantly.
>
> "I'm quitting," he said.
>
> "What's the trouble, Henry?"
>
> "Just this, I'm no salesman. I haven't got the nerve. I haven't got the ability, and I'm not worth the money you are paying me."
>
> There was something splendid about the courage of a man who would so frankly admit failure to his boss. He couldn't do that without nerve . . . To Henry's surprise, instead of accepting his resignation, I looked him squarely in the eye and said:
>
> "If I know how to pick men, you have sales stuff in you. I dare you, Henry Woods, to get out of this office, right now, and come back tonight with more orders than you have ever sold in any one day in your whole life."
>
> He looked at me dumfounded. Then a flash came into his eyes. It must have been the light of battle . . . He turned and walked out of my office.
>
> That night he came back. The defiant look of the early morning was replaced by the glow of victory. He had made the best record

of his life. He had beaten his best—and he has been beating his best ever since. (found in William H. Danforth, *I Dare You!*, St. Louis, MO: American Youth Foundation, 1991, 2–3.)

DARING PEOPLE TO BE THEIR BEST

As you may have concluded from the story I just cited, one of my favorite books is *I Dare You!* The author, William H. Danforth, was the founder and for many years the chairman of the board of the Ralston Purina Company. In this book, which he originally published as a limited edition for his family, business associates, and personal friends, he presented what he called fourfold development: think tall, stand tall, smile tall, and live tall. He called for people to "square up" their lives so that equal effort and energy were spent on the physical, mental, social,

> *As much as I applaud and appreciate those who have fire in the belly, if I have to make a choice between a person with good character and fire in the belly, I'll take character. A person with fire in the belly and no character is a wildfire about to be set.*

and religious aspects of life. Danforth invited his readers to dare themselves to become stronger physically—and he included posture illustrations so they might stand taller as well. He invited self-dares in the mental and social areas. I like his five social dares. They are very down to earth:

1. I dare you, Winning Smile, to replace Old Man Grouch.
2. I dare you, Mr. Snapping Turtle, to depart to another climate.
3. I dare you, Flabby Fingers, to develop into a Warm Handclasp.
4. I dare you, my own Personality, to become a Welcome Guest everywhere.
5. I dare you, my Social Self, to generate the Magnetic Spark which leads to a charmed life.

More people could benefit from making and pursuing these dares. I routinely dare people around me. I also dare the audiences to which I speak. I dare you . . .

. . . not to underestimate yourself. You can do more than you think you can.

. . . to be bigger than you are. You may be weak now, but you can become strong.

. . . to be one of the priceless few who goes in full pursuit of your own potential.

. . . to be adventuresome—always looking at life's problems as an opportunity for an adventure as you seek a solution.

. . . to go ahead and try—to believe you can do most anything, given the time and good instructions.

. . . to be strong. One of the most successful traits of any person is personal confidence and fortitude.

. . . to share. Ask yourself every day, "How can I help someone else?"

. . . to build character. I recommend the Bible as a book of principles to be learned and practiced.

. . . to spread Jesus' good news of God's love and forgiveness.

KEEPING THE FIRES BLAZING

I recently read a report citing that half of all workers in the United States are happy with their jobs—that means half are not! Only 14 percent of the people in this survey said they were "very satisfied" in their jobs. The survey was conducted nationally by the Conference Board, a market research firm in New York City. These numbers are part of a rather steady decline in job satisfaction over the last two decades.

This particular survey found that the greatest dissatisfaction was registered by workers who earned $25,000 to $35,000, and who were between the ages of thirty-five and forty-four. The three top reasons for their dissatisfaction were the rapid changes in technology, the employer's push for productivity, and shifting expectations about what a "good job" should be.

I dare you to be adventuresome— always looking at life's problems as an opportunity for an adventure as you seek a solution.

One conclusion of the researchers was especially interesting to me: "It's not just about money anymore. It's not about wages. It's about much more than that. It's about overall job aspects, both monetary and 'softer' issues as well."

Executives today—and tomorrow—will likely find themselves spending a great deal more time concerned about what it means to have satisfied employees.

At Pilgrim's Pride we've been concerned about this for decades—not just because it is expedient for maintaining a corporation, but because it's the right thing to do.

PILGRIM'S CARES

Our Partners know that I'm a Christian. I don't keep that a secret in the least. I don't insist that the people who work for me confess a personal faith in Jesus Christ, but I'm certainly pleased when they choose to do so. Pilgrim's Pride provides a chaplaincy program called Pilgrim's Cares to help people face life's difficult situations. The chaplains of that program are available to any Partner who might want an appointment. There's no hard sell for the gospel, but even so, about 5,000 of our Partners have voluntarily come to faith in Christ since we started this program in 1990. More than 3,600 have returned to church. The chaplains are also available for weddings, funerals, hospital visits, and just to listen or encourage our people and their familes at no charge to the employee. They are available twenty-four hours a day, every day of the week, and will help people whether they are on the job or at home. All conversations and visits are confidential.

Marketplace Ministries provides the chaplains, and this group has some 1,700 of their chaplains assigned to corporations nationwide. More than 250 of them serve our Partners. The chaplains have made more than 430,500 visits with our employees since 1990. At present we are paying them about $2 million a year—that's how committed we are to helping.

A COMMITMENT TO EDUCATION

Our deep commitment to education came out of the turbulent Sixties. Those were tremendous years of growth and impact for us, even though the nation as a whole seemed to be caught up in protests and dropping out of mainstream institutions and ideals:

- By 1966, we were producing 15 million broilers a year, 100,000 breeder hens, and 100,000 layers.
- We had moved from being a 100 percent bagged feed business in 1955 to a 90 percent bulk feed operation by 1966.
- We had built a new 130-by-134-foot hatchery that had the capacity to produce 300,000 chicks a week. It was completed in 1966.
- The Pilgrim Feed Mills name was officially registered with the state of Texas in 1968.
- By 1966, about 75 percent of our company's chicken production was being marketed in Los Angeles, California. We enjoyed a cost advantage over chickens produced on the West Coast.

To help deal with this changing environment, we developed a growing alliance with several schools and colleges. Our growth attracted a pilot program by the Midwest Feed Manufacturers Association, which brought educators and researchers to visit us. A delegation also came from Texas A&M University in search of a new approach to strengthen industry-university relations.

Enrollment had been dropping at agriculture schools despite a growing need for graduates in agribusiness and the numerous jobs available. It certainly was to our long-term benefit to see that more well-trained growers and others in agribusiness were being trained. From the university side, the results of university research projects—which were often more innovative and more scientifically rigorous than industry projects—remained largely unknown to many in agribusiness because of a lack of communication. We needed the skills and new information provided by the schools, and they needed our support in recruiting students. It was a win-win situation.

We began to give $10,000 scholarships to Poultry Science Department students at Texas A&M University.

Through the years, however, I recognized that college scholarships at that level, and in that specific field, weren't enough. Education needed to be more accessible to everybody who might be part of our workforce.

We developed a program to make education readily available to anybody in our company who desires to study. We don't limit the education of our employees to the acquisition of on-the-job skills. We also offer courses ranging from civics and government to personal finance. We have a tuition-reimbursement plan that pays for textbooks and tuition for Partners who wish to further their college education.

Since 2000, we have donated $3 million to educational pursuits, including $250,000 to pay for tuition for any student in rural Camp County to attend a local community college, which we have pledged to support.

NEVER STOP LEARNING

My early years had taught me to place high value on school, even though school in those days wasn't anything like what most young people have today.

The school in Pine was only about a quarter of a mile southeast from our home. I walked out my back door and across a field to get to the school, or I could walk out to the road and down the road to the school.

That was a little longer route, but after school, the walks along that road were a time of fellowship for about ten of us boys. The school didn't have any running water, but it had a pump outside. There were no fans.

I started school in Pine with first grade and went through the ninth grade there. Students in the tenth, eleventh, and twelfth grades attended high school in Pittsburg. I was among them. I didn't go to college, but I have sought to educate myself thoroughly in a number of disciplines. I place great value on higher learning.

We have found that those who give their time, talent, and energy to the community—and do so as a team—bring a much stronger team attitude back into the workplace. The good that is done in the company is a reflection of the good that is done in the community, and vice versa.

I have served as a member of the Dallas Baptist University Board of Trustees and was honored by DBU with the 1995 Russell H. Perry Free Enterprise Award. I have also received honorary degrees from three universities: a Doctor of Law degree from East Texas Baptist University, a Doctor of Humanities degree from Dallas Baptist University, and an Honorary Doctor of Philosophy degree from Stephen F. Austin State University.

Let's see . . . law . . . humanities . . . philosophy . . . and not one mention of agriculture or chickens! Seriously, I'm grateful for the opportunity to be associated with these fine institutions.

When I speak to young people today or to our employees, I often emphasize the importance of continuing to learn throughout life. I especially encourage people to:

- *Read more.* Make some of your reading nonfiction. Read about the lives of great people. Read the Bible in a version you have never read before. Read about something that captures your interest to the point that you'd like to "study up" on it.

This is a sketch of the home in which I grew up in Pine, Texas—the town's population was between 80 and 100 people. I enjoyed playing in the dirt under this house, making roadways with a make-believe truck fashioned out of an old roller skate.

I was named Lonnie after my father, Alonzo Pilgrim, but from birth, I was called "Bo." My father was a Christian, an entrepreneur, and a great dad—he was my hero. He died when I was 10 years old.

This wagon was my first "invention." I used it to haul bottles of Coke to sell to the workers at a business down the road from my father's general store.

I've always had a good sense of humor, lots of energy, and a high degree of confidence—traits I see in this childhood "school" photo of myself (back row, far right).

You CAN TELL A GOOD SOLDIER BY HIS SALUTE

I served in the military during the Korean War. I was always taught that you can tell a good soldier by his salute. In life as a whole, I believe strongly that you can tell a good man by looking at Who he salutes!

I'm standing on the porch of the first feed store that my brother Aubrey and I operated together, beginning in 1946—a far cry but only a few miles away from the new world headquarters building for the Pilgrim's Pride Corporation that has sales of $5 billion-plus a year.

I still enjoying riding in the "ChickFest" parade in my hometown of Pittsburg, Texas—with Henrietta and my Pilgrim hat. This truck is similar to the one I drove for Aubrey at our first feed store.

In the 1980s I became a master at cooking chicken chili at countless fairs and exhibitions. I've never been bashful about promoting my own products—they're the BEST!

At Pilgrim's Pride, we hatch 6.5 million chickens a DAY. That's a fact that I like to "crow" about.

Private jet travel out of an airstrip near our world headquarters building in the rural East Texas town of Pittsburg allows me to stay in personal touch with our many plants and distribution centers across the United States and in Mexico and Puerto Rico. In each of our three corporate jets I have placed a Bible with the inscription, "Jesus, thank You for the plane."

My wife Patty and I were privileged to donate a Prayer Tower at the central square of our hometown of Pittsburg, Texas. Visitors have come from around the world. The tower chimes hymns each evening.

I threw out the first pitch at a Texas Rangers game . . . but I think the fans enjoyed more my cackling and "strutting my stuff" with the San Diego Chicken that day.

Patty and I were honored to share the stage with President Bush and his family during George W. Bush's campaign for governor of Texas. We hosted the Bush family at our home—they were delightful guests, and we had a great time.

I've been married for more than forty-nine years to Patty (Redding) Pilgrim, one of the sweetest and most beautiful women I've ever known.

This is our home in Pittsburg, Texas.

The new Pilgrim's Pride Corporation World Headquarters Park
in Pittsburg, Texas, was completed in April 2005.

- *Develop a notebook habit.* Have a pen and paper within reach at all times. Jot down original ideas as you have them. Take notes in meetings and at special conferences and church services. What you write down you are far more likely to remember and to act upon. Keep a notepad and pen by your bed at night. Many people awaken in the night with a good idea, but that idea has evaporated by morning. Take a few seconds to jot down the middle-of-the-night idea. It may be a winner!
- *Learn to listen.* Everybody with good hearing can hear. It takes effort to listen intently as if you will be responsible for repeating verbatim what you have heard. You can't ever really learn something from another person until you first learn to listen to that person.

A Program to Reflect Community Pride

In addition to giving our Partners opportunities in education and helping them through counseling, we give them an opportunity to become involved in charities and volunteer work. We call the program "Company and Community Pride." We have found that those who give their time, talent, and energy to the community—and do so as a team—bring a much stronger team attitude back into the workplace. The good that is done in the company is a reflection of the good that is done in the community, and vice versa.

Opportunities to Celebrate Together

We like to celebrate our milestones at Pilgrim's Pride. We had a major celebration when we turned fifty years old as a company. The year was 1996. Sales and capacity utilization were at all-time highs and generating record results. Production and operating efficiencies were also at all-time highs. It was time to celebrate! We went to Six Flags Over Texas in

Arlington on September 9. We leased more than 150 buses to transport our Partners and growers to the Six Flags park for this special occasion. The company paid for more than 12,500 Partners and their family members to enjoy the day. And in something of a grand finale fashion, we gave away cash door prizes of $1,000, $2,500, $5,000, and $10,000—all after-tax figures.

Partners who celebrate together stay together.

★　★　★

Whatever you want men to do to you,
do also to them.
(Matt. 7:12 NKJV)

9

THE CHALLENGE OF
CONTINUOUS IMPROVEMENT

Mickey Bradshaw, who is retired now, was in charge of our wholesale feed division for a number of years. He liked to tell the people who worked for him what I had said to him one morning. I had gone to his office and asked how things were going. Mickey said, "I have a lot of problems!" I replied to him, "Good! If it weren't for problems, I wouldn't need you," and left his office.

Mickey used that same line with the people on his team. He came to expect them to be problem solvers, just as I had expected him to be a problem solver.

I believe it's much healthier if those at the top look down the corporate ladder for solutions. The people who are living and working with the problems are very likely the people who know the most about a problem and have an idea how it can best be fixed. Their ideas need to be heard!

In many corporations, people look up the corporate ladder for solutions to problems. I believe it's much healthier if those at the top look down the corporate ladder for solutions. The people who are living and working with the problems are very likely the people who know the most about a problem and have an idea how it can best be fixed. Their ideas need to be heard!

Problem solving is at the heart of our management philosophy, which is summed up in two words: *Continuous Improvement*.

These two words embody what I believe should be a motivating drive for every person. If you aren't moving forward, you're falling behind. If you aren't growing, you're declining. If you aren't living more abundantly, you're dying slowly.

We should be in continuous improvement in every area of life.

At Pilgrim's Pride, our management style and business philosophy is named Continuous Improvement and is based on fourteen guidelines. I'm happy to share them with you. These points are adapted from Dr. W. Edwards Deming's book, *Out of the Crisis* (MIT Press, 1982). Deming is considered the father of the quality movement. We've been putting these guidelines into practice since 1991, and they work.

1. *Have a constancy of purpose.* We seek to improve our products and services so we can be competitive, stay in business, and provide jobs. The business process starts with the customer, and everything else is designed from there. We don't stray from our purpose.

2. *Adopt a new style of management.* Continuous Improvement *is* our management style.

3. *Cease dependence on inspection.* We have learned to reduce dependence on inspection on a mass basis by building quality into the product or service in the first place. Managing outcomes by detecting defects, then reworking the defective products is the old and expensive way of doing business.

4. *Avoid doing business on price tag alone.* We seek to minimize our total costs, but sometimes the best way to a low total cost means not using cheap products or doing things the cheapest way.

5. *Seek continuous improvement of processes.* The best way to improve quality and productivity, and thus constantly decrease total cost, is to continually improve the processes that produce the products and services.

6. *Train and retrain.* Every person must be trained to be an expert at his or her job. Training is the cornerstone of greater consistency.

7. *Improvement of leadership.* Leaders are required. Leaders have a responsibility to improve the system, not just manage an old system. Leaders engage in coaching, teaching, and motivating. Leaders don't merely find and record failures but seek to remove the causes of failures.

8. *Drive out fear.* Preconceived fears and negative emotions from previous experiences and jobs can hinder progress. So can fear of failure— which tends to lead to mediocrity. Leaders need to recognize that the elimination of fear takes time and attention, but is of tremendous benefit.

9. *Departments must work together.* Not only does a company benefit from vertical integration, but it benefits greatly when departments are cross-functional and work in an integrated way. Everyone must get involved in innovation and work to create an atmosphere of mutual respect and trust.

10. *Continuous Improvement provides its own motivation.* Motivation comes when a person is in a highly charged, exciting environment in which every person is encouraged to be successful, to reach his or her potential, and to try new ideas.

11. *Work standards and quotas shall not limit performance.* Work standards tend to cap the amount of improvement that can be achieved. They have a limiting effect. In truth, there is no limit to what can be achieved in a continuously improving organization. A new idea, a new technology, or a new process can always take an organization to a higher level.

12. *Remove barriers that rob Partners of their right to pride of workmanship.* Stress quality, not sheer numbers. Examine *every* system and procedure to see if it supports or inhibits continuous improvement. Respect people as the organization's most valuable resource. Focus on the outcomes that lead to optimal performance and exceed customer needs.

13. *Institute education and self-improvement.* Help Partners become more educated and better trained. Improve their lives as well as their work skills. People have the potential to renew themselves, and education is an investment in personal renewal.

14. *Do it!* Don't wait until you feel motivated to engage in Continuous Improvement . . . do it! Don't wait until you feel like putting these principles into effect or until your boss insists that you do . . . do it! Don't wait until your coworkers lead the way . . . do it! Responsibility for Continuous Improvement cannot be delegated. It begins and ends with a person taking on that responsibility for himself or herself.

Continuous Improvement is focused on how we do our jobs. It's a perspective that is aimed first and foremost at quality and adding value to everything we do—in other words, improving every aspect of our products and processes to achieve real excellence. Continuous Improvement is focused on the goal of meeting our customers' needs and creating products for them that are what they want, at the price that makes it valuable to them, delivered on time to their place of business. Continuous Improvement is a means of identifying, quantifying, and eliminating waste. It's about doing a better job and then a better job and then a still better job.

Doing things in a high-quality way is ultimately cost-effective because it means that you have far fewer "do-overs" and produce far fewer leftovers.

Practically speaking, we routinely keep Process Analysis Worksheets in which we evaluate various suppliers and customers. Here are the questions we ask:

- *Suppliers.* Who are your suppliers? Are they meeting your requirements?
- *Customers.* Who are your customers? What are their requirements? Are you meeting their requirements?
- *Improvements.* How can this process be improved?
- *Value.* How does this process add value?

When our Partners point out problems to us, we also invite them to come up with as many possible solutions as they can envision and then tell us which of them they believe to be the best solution and why. As part of our commitment to our Partners, we ask management to provide an action plan related to the problem and suggested solution.

BELIEFS ARE ADDED
TO CONTINUOUS IMPROVEMENT

The goals of Continuous Improvement are very task oriented. At the root of these goals must be a foundation of basic beliefs—specifically beliefs that the company holds from the top down. Beliefs infuse hope. They give a perspective for making management choices. They provide a framework for respecting every Partner's contribution to the team, and every Partner's ability to pursue Continuous Improvement.

We have identified and adopted ten Basic Belief statements. They are added to the concepts of Continuous Improvement, and they have been in effect at Pilgrim's Pride for a number of years. I am happy to share them with you because they also work!

1. *The customer's needs are critical.* The customer needs to be the focus of all company activities. Customer satisfaction is critical to success.

2. *Anything can be improved.* All processes, products, and services can be made better.

3. *Quality is* everyone's *job.* Quality products and services are the results of quality processes and quality work. To leave any person out of the process or to accept anything less than excellence is to miss an opportunity to improve.

4. *The person doing the job knows it best.* Nobody knows a job like the person who does it every day. If that isn't true, the person needs more training.

5. *People deserve respect.* Every person in the organization must feel valued and important.

6. *Teamwork works.* Synergy is the concept that says one plus one equals more than two. That's what happens in good teamwork.

7. *There is value in differences.* The earth would be a horrible and boring place if everybody was the same. We all have unique backgrounds, skills, and experiences. Differences are healthy and promote creativity and a productive exchange of ideas. Without differences, we wouldn't have new ideas.

8. *Involvement builds commitment.* People are more motivated to act when they have had a say in deciding what action to take.

9. *Support builds success.* When workers assist and encourage one another, everybody has a greater opportunity to succeed.

10. You *make the difference.* An organization is only as good as the individual people who staff it. Every person affects quality, costs, productivity, and customer satisfaction. Everyone makes a difference.

Taken as a whole, our statements of Continuous Improvement and Basic Beliefs stress teamwork, a focus on customer needs, and empowerment of Partners to seek long-term solutions that might increase productivity, prevent waste, and encourage higher quality—especially in areas that do not rely upon inspection but depend upon using the best processes and procedures. Our objectives for Continuous Improvement are related specifically to profits, job satisfaction, and customer satisfaction—all of which can be verified statistically. In other words, we all have a clear idea about the degree to which we are improving continuously.

Every job is a process—people who hold jobs are always capable of improving, growing, adapting to new technologies, and achieving higher levels of excellence. We want Partners to be fully engaged in each of these processes. Not only is it good for the company and ultimately the bottom line, but it is more fulfilling and satisfying to the individual.

I don't know any person who dislikes learning—sometimes change is difficult, but if you put change in the context of growth, it becomes enjoyable and ultimately rewarding. I strongly believe that people like to feel fulfilled by their jobs—to know that they've put in a good day's work for a good day's pay. I certainly wouldn't do what I do without that sense of fulfillment and satisfaction.

A REFLECTION OF HIGH VALUE

Value is a significant word for us at Pilgrim's Pride. So is the phrase *long-term working relationship*. These words are especially important as they relate to our customers and suppliers.

I strongly believe people want to be valued and needed, and have an opportunity to give to others. Our Creator built something into us that few people in business seem to understand: people need to be needed. They want their contributions to count, but they also want their *presence* to count.

Valuing people seems to be something that rural and small-town Americans understand a little better than city folk, at least from my perspective. We have a saying here in Pittsburg that you can recognize a person from behind—which means

> *I strongly believe that people like to feel fulfilled by their jobs—to know that they've put in a good day's work for a good day's pay. I certainly wouldn't do what I do without that sense of fulfillment and satisfaction.*

that even if you see only his back, you know who he is by name. You probably know some of his family members and a little about his personal life. You are likely to know where he lives.

Every person might not be your best friend, but there's a strong sense in our town that every person *counts*. Every person needs to have a roof over his or her head, food on the table, a good school for the children, a job that provides adequate income, and a friendly greeting when you meet the person on the street or over the counter at a local diner. Nobody is "just a number."

Now, it doesn't really matter what the person does as his or her job—as long as it's legal and moral. What matters is that the person has a job because a job makes a person feel like a contributing member of the community—not just as a taxpayer, although that is important, but as someone who is helping to create an improved quality of life for a family and community.

What is true for us in the community of Pittsburg is what I hope is established in every facility that bears the name Pilgrim's Pride—whether it's a chicken house operation, a processing plant, a hatchery, a feed mill, or a farm store. People need to be valued because *who* they are is just as important to the overall environment of the workplace as *what* they produce.

I want our Partners to do just what I encourage my managers and top executives to do—freely express ideas and suggestions so together we can find better ways of doing jobs that benefit the company. Many decisions made by the company in the last couple of decades have come out of work teams of hourly Partners.

If any process in our company adds value, we should improve it. If it doesn't add value, we should eliminate it.

Two Things We Monitor Continually

There are two things that we seek to monitor continually throughout the company: training and fear elimination.

TRAINING

When it comes to producing quality in any process or procedure, the starting point is always education and training. You can't expect a person to do quality work if the person hasn't been trained to do quality work— to know the standards for good quality, to know how to do the tasks related to the work, and to become skilled enough at the job to do it well every time, countless times. A person can grow and continue to improve only if he or she is given sufficient knowledge and understanding of every new innovation or piece of equipment that comes along.

FEAR ELIMINATION

I've met people who run faster or fight harder when they are afraid, but I've never met people who genuinely work better when they are afraid, at least not for very long. Fear adds pressure and distraction to any process.

No fear of management. I don't want anybody in my company to be afraid of management. In fact, we have a toll-free hotline where any issue can be raised anonymously.

I don't purposefully set out to be accessible or visible in the company or in my community because I'm trying to manage through my managers. But the fact is, I am very accessible and visible in Pilgrim's Pride facilities and in my hometown because I'm just that kind of guy.

I've met people who run faster or fight harder when they are afraid, but I've never met people who genuinely work better when they are afraid, at least not for very long. Fear adds pressure and distraction to any process.

I enjoy meeting with friends for Saturday morning coffee at a local restaurant; we've been meeting that way for years. That's part of friendship—to meet, to talk, to share our lives, to exchange a few bits of information and a few good jokes. I teach a Sunday School class at my church. Again, I've been doing that for years. I sometimes tell people, "If you want to get to know me better, come on over to my Sunday School class. You'll discover what I believe and who I believe in, and these are the most important things you can know about Bo Pilgrim."

Just about the last thing in the world I'd ever want to see happen would be to see Partners cower or back away from me in fear. That reaction wouldn't be their fault—it would be my fault. It's up to the leader, and to the executives and managers, to set a tone that every person can be approached, especially if a problem or a suggestion for improvement is involved.

No fear of change. Partners need to have the assurance that if things change, they still have a valued role to play. From my experience, people resist change only if they see it as a threat to their survival. Nobody wants to have his job outsourced or eliminated—but even if that has to happen from time to time, an employee can be made to feel confident that he or she will be trained for a new job within the company or will be given assistance in finding another opportunity outside the company.

Again, I think this is probably a reflection of my life spent in the same small community. Technologies come and go. Jobs come and go. The people of Pittsburg and other similar rural communities tend to stay. They get used to new technologies and take on new jobs. The workforce doesn't change—rather, the tasks done by the workforce change.

No fear of failing. Nobody gets everything right every time. But we can train people who work with us to make as few mistakes as possible. How? By fully training them in how to do a job, fully informing them about what is expected of them, and fully helping them to conquer new skills and learn new information. If a person is failing at a job, it probably isn't the person's fault as much as it is the fault of the one responsible for doing the training.

Certainly there are lazy people. There are also people that the Bible calls "one talent" people—they might be more limited in what they are able to learn and do. But the greater truth is that lazy people can be motivated to work and "one talent" people can be put in a position where their one talent is extremely useful.

If people are challenged to learn something new, they need to be challenged to believe they can learn the new skill and be successful at it.

No fear of losing a job. If a Partner is fired, that's far more likely to be a fault of the company than the fault of the employee, at least in many corporations I've witnessed over the years. It may be that the employee wasn't given clear enough directives, good enough safety systems, strong enough motivation, adequate training, or enough person-to-person supervision. It may be that the company wasn't wise in hiring the person in the first place—or perhaps not wise in hiring the person to fill the particular position he or she was assigned.

Firing a person is very serious business to me. I know that I'm affecting not only that person, but also his family, his reputation in the community, his ability to contribute to his church and the town in which he lives, and his future employability. Losing a job is extremely demoralizing and can put some people into a tailspin that's hard to pull out of. I'm all for giving a Partner a second chance whenever possible—and sometimes a third chance. We believe in progressive discipline when there are performance issues. And in return, I expect a diligent effort to put in a good day's work, honesty and integrity, and truthfulness on the part of the Partner.

I intend to treat the people who work with me with the basics of good character—and I expect to be treated that way.

Most people I know want a job in which their employer is concerned about the character and integrity of the employees—that sends a signal that the employer is a person of character and integrity, and that the overall work environment is going to be pleasant over the long haul.

Motivating Standards and Quotas

A person who is well trained, and is unafraid of change, failure, and job loss, is likely to be far more motivated by high work standards and quotas instead of being intimidated by them. Through the years, I've rarely met a person who didn't want to do his best and to do well in the eyes of others. We all want to feel that we can attain success if we use our skills and knowledge to the best of our ability. Every person wants to be an expert at what he does—to have the satisfaction of knowing that he's good at his job and is valued.

When a person is appreciated and given the opportunity to succeed, that person rarely backs down in the face of a higher standard of excellence. To the contrary! He wants to achieve it because he believes he can, knows he will be rewarded for his accomplishment, and knows he will have increased satisfaction that he is a person of value. He wants to believe there are no limits to what he can do and become.

I know that's true in my life. I have a strong hunch it's true for 99.9 percent of those who work for Pilgrim's Pride—and even for the untold millions of people who don't have that privilege.

A CORPORATE WAY OF LIFE

I suppose that Continuous Improvement might be considered just another management program in some companies, one aimed at improving quality. We consider it an overall philosophy that is really more like a way of life.

When a person is appreciated and given the opportunity to succeed, that person rarely backs down in the face of a higher standard of excellence.

Good training and education make a person competent and productive.

Good courage—the absence of a fear of failure—makes a person willing to take the risk of trying something new, adapting to something different, and succeeding at something he or she has never accomplished before.

That is true not only in the corporate environment, but in every neighborhood, every church, and every school.

Show me any group of people who are doing their utmost to become informed and skilled, and who have great courage when it comes to innovation, new standards of excellence, and new technology, and I'll show you a group of people who are going someplace. If they are people of good character with good purpose, they are going someplace great.

I like smart, skilled, bold people. They are the people who really make this world hum.

★   ★   ★

Let us not grow weary while doing good,
for in due season we shall reap if we do not lose heart.
(Gal. 6:9 NKJV)

10

A Noble Mission of
Saving Rural North America

Even though we rely upon agricultural production just as much as we ever have in the United States, the overall trend is one of fewer and fewer people shouldering the burden of producing agricultural products. In 1935, there were nearly 7 million farms in the United States, more than at any other time in our country's history. But by 2002, the number of farms had dropped to 2.1 million.

The average farm today is much larger than it was in 1935, and certainly technology has greatly helped farmers produce far more food per acre than they did seventy years ago. Still, there are fewer and fewer farmers left every year, and there are a lot more people to feed, both here at home and around the world. Even so, the number of farms in the *poultry* business is actually increasing.

Especially in East Texas, where our headquarters are located, we have seen a growth in the number of poultry farms. I take tremendous satisfaction in knowing that we are helping families remain in smaller towns and rural areas. I am deeply committed to saving a rural lifestyle in the United States, as well as in Puerto Rico and Mexico.

Pilgrim's Pride has major facilities in Texas, Alabama, Arkansas, Georgia, Kentucky, Louisiana, North Carolina, Pennsylvania, Tennessee, Virginia, West Virginia, Puerto Rico, and Mexico—and some other facilities in Arizona, California, Iowa, Mississippi, Utah, and Wisconsin.

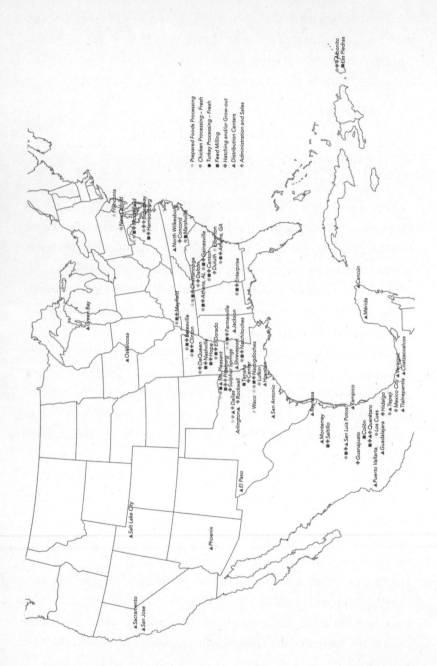

Prepared Foods Processing
Chicken Processing – Fresh
Turkey Processing – Fresh
Feed Milling
Hatching and/or Grow-out
Distribution Centers
Administration and Sales

I have included a map that shows our locations. Why share this with you? Because I'm guessing that most readers have never heard of these places! The vast majority of our plants are in small towns. When you have some 1,500 Partners in a place like De Queen, Arkansas, you are a major player in town—and for me personally, I feel a tremendous responsibility to these Partners because I know that the success of Pilgrim's Pride enables them to remain in a small town and still succeed economically.

Some facilities are union facilities, others are nonunion, and some are a mix—for example, the facility in Aibonito, Puerto Rico, has a nonunion processing facility and a unionized feed mill. The workers are the ones who decide about union matters. In some areas, unions have been perceived to be a plus to the workers, while in other areas, workers have decided to work without unionization.

Having a goal of saving rural North America generates two questions:

1. *How do we intend to do this?* Our corporate statement of purpose says it well: create jobs through the production of healthy and economical chicken, turkey, and egg products for the rest of the world.

The main reason that people from small towns leave their roots—their hometowns and the farms on which they grew up—is that they can't make a good living in the country. In other words, they can't earn enough money in their small business to feed their families and educate their children; they can't make enough money farming to pay for equipment, seed, feed, and land mortgages; or they can't find a job. These three problems are fixable ones, in my opinion. I'm very concerned that the people in small towns

- stay employed;
- make sufficient money to adequately support their families and pay their bills; and
- have sufficient money to sustain their property and support their communities so they can pass on this heritage to the next generation.

Rural America will be saved, to a great extent, by the creation of good-paying jobs that allow young men and women of talent, intelligence, and skill to stay in rural America and make a good living. I am very proud of the fact that I was chosen in 1987 as East Texan of the Year primarily for providing jobs in East Texas.

A few years later, CNBC aired a nationally televised series of programs, *Profiles of America*, that focused on successful American businesses. Pilgrim's Pride had thirty minutes of coverage in a program describing the positive impact that we have on sustaining rural life in the United States and Mexico.

There's nothing that says a chicken hatched and raised in a rural environment needs to be processed at, cooked in, or distributed from a plant in a rural area. Chickens travel well in trucks. We have made a concerted effort, however, to keep the processing, cooking, and distribution jobs as close to the farm as possible.

Doing this isn't always easy, however. As much as I love small-town and rural American life—and wouldn't personally relocate for any reason—not everything about small-town and rural America is necessarily convenient or easy when it comes to corporate growth.

Let me give you an example.

In the mid-1980s customers sent a strong signal to us that they wanted more fully cooked and further-processed products—meat portions that were ready to pick up, heat up, and eat up. Everything in our research indicated that this was a growing trend, not a fad. Americans are busier than ever, and they like high-quality products that they can prepare at home almost as fast as stopping by the drive-through lane at a fast-food restaurant. We knew we needed to act quickly to lead the way in addressing this market interest, and the means of doing that involved expanding our operations to add an ultramodern chicken cooking facility. Fortunately we had financial partners who were able to step up to the challenge—and quickly.

The chicken-cooking facility needed to be located close to or adjacent to a processing plant, which would supply chickens to the new cooking facility. And we needed to hire additional employees for the processing and cooking operations. All these factors create, as you can easily imagine, something of a balancing act: where to locate a new operation so as to have employees who can staff it! Small towns are small towns. There are only so many available employees even if every available adult is working in a plant. Pittsburg is only about ten miles from Mount Pleasant, a larger community, but our major processing and distribution plants were already in Mount Pleasant. We began to search for a location that would allow us to draw from Pittsburg, Mount Pleasant, and other small towns—close enough to the Pittsburg feed mill, hatcheries, and chicken houses. We settled on Mount Pleasant as the location for our state-of-the-art Prepared Foods facility.

In some cases, adaptation has meant adding Saturday shifts in order to increase processing capacity. In most small towns, Saturday is something of a family and community day—that's when special events are scheduled, sidewalk sales are conducted, and people tend to watch their loved ones perform in everything from community theater productions to Little League games. There's a special motivational challenge in getting people to work on Saturday and take a different day off.

The challenges are there. Just being rural doesn't mean being easier. So . . .

2. *Why have a goal of saving rural North America?* Because rural America is a wonderful place to live and raise children and be together as families!

Rural America is a place where friendships run long and caring runs deep.

Rural America is a place where people know their neighbors and take care of them. I go to Dallas fairly often—it is only about one hundred-twenty miles away from Pittsburg—and I'm aware that there are countless hundreds of homeless people in Dallas. For the most part, they seem to be faceless, nameless people that everybody expects the government or a social services agency to feed and shelter. There are very few homeless people that I know about in Pittsburg, Texas. If someone comes to town without a job and is willing to work, work can be found for that person. If someone is unable to work or care for himself in a time of physical illness or material loss, neighbors help out. If someone needs a roof over her head, a way can be found to find that person a place to call "home." If someone loses his shirt, someone gives that person a shirt. Rural Americans take care of their own.

Rural America is also a place of great faith. If a person doesn't show up at church on a Sunday morning, neighbors call to see whether there's a problem. If a person doesn't go to church at all, someone comes calling with an invitation to attend. If a person wants to get involved in a church, there's always a place of service for that person!

Rural America is a place where people know their mayor and city council representatives by name. In my hometown, we've had the same mayor for more than five decades. Virtually everybody in Pittsburg knows Mayor D. H. Abernathy, and he makes himself approachable and available to listen to people and respond to their needs. If he's not in his office, you can probably find him at a local diner—and his secretary will probably tell you which one. The people in rural America tend to know their state legislators and congressmen—by reputation and family affiliation, if not personally. They know the school board leaders, the sheriff, the chief of police, the fire chief, and other people of community service on a first-name basis. Rural Americans have a "smaller world" when it comes to population; therefore, they have more impact when it comes to taking part in school-related issues, volunteer organizations, business organizations, arts groups, and community projects.

Rural America is a place where a person's character and reputation are more valuable than the job title or the bank balance. A person may not have much money or status but still be called a "good man" or a "fine woman." Honesty, hard work, morality, kindness, generosity, friendliness, and integrity are prized.

Certainly not everybody in rural America is squeaky clean or morally upright. Every community has people who are derelict—at least once in a while. Every community has people who break the law, are lazy, or won't work very hard or long at a given job. The difference is that rural Americans tend to confront these people when they need to be confronted, and also to accommodate these people as part of the community. Those who get drunk are given a place to sleep it off, and those who are lazy are prodded into doing something productive under the old proverb, "Those who work, eat." People aren't just given a second chance; in some cases, they are given a second hundredth chance. Why? Because that person is likely to be a childhood friend, the son or daughter of a former Sunday School teacher, or the grandchild of a person who befriended you when you were a youngster.

> *Rural America is a place where a person's character and reputation are more valuable than the job title or the bank balance. A person may not have much money or status but still be called a "good man" or a "fine woman." Honesty, hard work, morality, kindness, generosity, friendliness, and integrity are prized.*

Certainly not everybody in rural America is equally talented or intelligent. There are just as many sick, elderly, unskilled, and uneducated people in rural America—percentage wise—as in suburbs and cities. The difference is that rural America seems to regard the chronically sick and the elderly as part of the fabric of life—they are cared for, not shuttled off to a center of some type where strangers care for their needs. If people want or need training or education, they usually can find somebody willing to show them the ropes or give them an opportunity.

The vast majority of our Partners live in small towns. Their roots give them a sense of place and an appreciation for the feel and rhythm of life in small-town America. They have a deep, bred-in-the-bone knowledge of what small towns need—and one of the foremost things they need is good jobs. They work regular hours and have good opportunities for advancement. They receive good benefits and salaries that exceed minimum wage, even for new hires.

As a result, they take pride in their work, their company, and themselves. They take ownership of the products they produce.

Rural America is where I've chosen to live my life. It's a place I value highly and want to see flourish.

A Hometown Is a Place to Which You Give Back

I've lived in Pittsburg almost sixty years and in Camp County, where both Pittsburg and Pine are located, all my life.

Pittsburg has a population of just over four thousand people. Located in Northeast Texas, it is surrounded by fields, forests, and six lakes. The town is an old one by Texas standards. It was founded by Major William Harrison Pitts who came to Texas from Georgia in 1854. He bought two hundred acres of wilderness from the state of Texas for sixty cents an acre and set aside fifty of those acres for a town site. Pitts and his followers grew cotton, which they hauled by wagon forty-eight miles southeast to Jefferson where riverboats floated the bales down to the Red River and on to market in New Orleans.

On the streets of Pittsburg, life moves slowly. The downtown district has had eighteen of its aging storefronts lovingly restored, and the community spirit is strong. Inside our corporate headquarters, life moves at a slightly quicker pace, but people are still friendly! Heritage, hospitality, and hot links all have a strong history in Pittsburg—Pittsburg Hot Links are famous in this part of Texas, but poultry is the heart of the local economy.

Most hours of most days you can find a Pilgrim's Pride truck rolling through the streets of the town or train cars being unloaded at the feed mill.

I like living in Pittsburg. It's an easy place to call home.

And I'm a firm believer in giving back to one's town. Patty and I created a park in downtown Pittsburg in the early 1990s.

I bought the property for this park, by the way, from a man I've known since high school days, James Sewell. His father sold a bicycle to my brother on credit—it was my first bicycle. James's father had a parts business, and James turned it into a marine business that also handled lawnmowers. James and I were on the board of deacons at our church together. Through the years, James and his family acquired a number of pieces of property in the central part of town. I bought a lot from him years ago. And then I waited twenty years for him to sell me a second lot! I gave both pieces of property to our church for expansion. That's the way things are done in a small town—friends work together, worship together, and buy and sell from each other.

We named the park we created at the center of town Witness Park. In the midst of it is a Prayer Tower that we built as a distinctive landmark for the community. Above the chapel is a seventy-five-foot chiming bell tower supporting four Paccard bells made in France. The chapel is always open, and it offers a place of quiet refuge for the town's citizens and visitors. The guest register there tells us that we have had visitors from around the world.

In the chapel, four stained-glass windows depict the life of Jesus. The structure cost Patty and me $1.5 million personally, but it was worth every penny. It was dedicated on Easter Sunday 1992.

In the neighboring town of Mount Pleasant, our company gave a $1.4 million grant for the city to build a 62.8-acre park that has tennis, basketball, and volleyball courts, softball fields, a soccer field, concession stands, a pavilion, and a half-mile walking trail around a three-acre lake.

Why do these things?

Because we're concerned about the quality of life in the towns where we live and do most of our business. It's a way of giving back. It's a way of saying "thank you." The park in Mount Pleasant is called Heritage Park, and that about sums it up. Giving something back to a community is a way of establishing heritage. In fact, our Partners are well known for their caring spirit all across the seventeen U.S. states where we do business, as well as Puerto Rico and Mexico. Thousands of our people give of their time and money to help make our communities better places to live and work.

THE PILGRIM BANK

Another way we have chosen to give back to Pittsburg may be less obvious to some people—Pilgrim Bank. We were not motivated primarily by the prospect of making money when we started Pilgrim Bank, although a good banker must be concerned with making money if a bank is to remain operational.

For years, the main bank in Pittsburg had a ceiling on the amount of money that would be loaned to any one customer for personal reasons. That ceiling was high enough for a person to purchase a car or a boat perhaps. It was usually not high enough for a person to finance a home or a small business—especially as the costs of housing and doing business rose with inflation. We didn't initiate any form of takeover in the situation. Rather, we waited until the time came when the owners of the bank wanted to sell. We made a bid on the bank, and thus, I became not only a chicken man, but also a banker. I still serve as chairman of Pilgrim Bank, which now has five locations in Pittsburg and Mount Pleasant, Texas. I've been the majority owner and served on the bank's board of directors since 1969. The bank serves a trade territory of several counties in Northeast Texas.

The bank is directly across the street from the Prayer Tower and its park, and from the church I attend, First Baptist Church in Pittsburg. I like the geographic proximity of these facilities. In a wonderful way, the spiritual and material aspects of my life seem linked.

It has always been more important to me to know how to live than how to make a living. I don't believe money should be separated from a person's spiritual life—the way we handle money is a very good indicator of the way we handle all of God's gifts to us. Furthermore, money is one of the main means by which we can bless other people and share the gospel with those who don't know Christ Jesus. Money is meant to be *given* and *invested*. I do both. And I like to do both in rural America whenever possible!

It has always been more important to me to know how to live than how to make a living. I don't believe money should be separated from a person's spiritual life—the way we handle money is a very good indicator of the way we handle all of God's gifts to us.

★　★　★

If you diligently obey the voice of the LORD your God,
to observe carefully all His commandments which I command
you today . . . Blessed shall you be in the city, and
blessed shall you be in the country.
(Deut. 28:1, 3 NKJV)

II

Our Expansion into Mexico

All things considered, it would be a lot easier for me, and for Pilgrim's Pride, to remain in the United States and simply sell products here, rather than run plants and distribution in other nations. Our main reason for going into Old Mexico was not just to make money, although any good businessperson has to be concerned with the bottom line of any operation.

I had been in Mexico enough to know that many people in rural Mexico were poor, and they also had a lack of meat protein in their diet.

I wanted to see the chicken business help Mexico in the same way I had seen it help rural parts of the United States—by providing an affordable, high-quality source of protein for the common man, and adding to the prosperity of the people who worked the farms. As the years passed, I became increasingly concerned about the health and economic welfare of our neighbors in Mexico.

Part of this concern is also rooted in my belief that when our near neighbors are well-fed and economically stable, we will have far fewer immigration problems in the United States, much stronger allies, and a stronger consumer base for all American products, including poultry.

In 1987 we negotiated the acquisition of three companies in Mexico. One was Nutricos of Mexico City, which had operations in Queretaro, Tepeji del Rio, and Mexico City. Another was purchased from Mexico's director of poultry in the agricultural department at the time, Dr. Enrique

Salinas. The third company, privately owned by Hugo Martinez, was located in San Luis Potosi.

Doing business in Mexico involved forging an agreement with the Mexican government, and also the U.S. Foreign Investment Commission, so we might purchase Mexican debt from the First National Bank of Chicago through an equity swap. We paid fifty-three cents on the dollar for this government debt, and Mexico, in turn, paid the owners for the three operations that we wanted to buy. The deal closed in January 1988 with Pilgrim's Pride paying more than $20 million for the operations, minus the discount.

Our agreement with the Foreign Investment Commission stated that all the profits for the first three years would be spent in Mexico to modernize the facilities there.

In 1988 we added several Purina farms to our Mexico holdings, and in May of 1989 we purchased the Purina Feed Mill in Queretaro, Mexico. We needed the additional mill because our chicken business was growing so rapidly in Mexico.

With these acquisitions, we became a player in international agribusiness.

In the next three years, we tripled the size of our operations in Mexico. By 1991, we had more than 400 chicken houses (with approximately 8 million square feet) and a new hatchery in Mexico. Our processing capacity had doubled.

Today we operate three chicken-processing plants and eighteen distribution centers in Mexico, and our operations there are strategically located to serve 75 percent of all Mexican consumers.

THE CHALLENGE OF DOING
BUSINESS INTERNATIONALLY

One of the things I've learned about competing in the worldwide marketplace is this: to be successful you have to be better than the best.

Another thing I've learned is that the rules for doing business here in the United States aren't necessarily the same as the rules for doing business in other nations. For example, about 20 percent of what we produce in Mexico is termed *New York–dressed,* which means the viscera are still in the bird, and the head and feet are attached. At one point that percentage was as high as 80 percent. These types of chickens do not appear in U.S. supermarkets these days. Overall, the product mix in Mexico also includes 8 percent grocery store whole birds, almost 30 percent rotisserie birds without the giblets, and 26 percent parts of birds.

Furthermore, in some parts of Mexico the customers want a white bird without skin and fat, but many customers still want a yellow-skinned bird because they believe it is healthier. To keep our chickens nutritionally sound, but add nonfat yellow color to them, we feed the birds yellow corn and marigold, which adds about five cents a pound to the cost of raising a bird. About half of our birds in Mexico are fed for yellow color, and the other half are grown white.

> *The rules for doing business here in the United States aren't necessarily the same as the rules for doing business in other nations. For example, about 20 percent of what we produce in Mexico is termed New York–dressed, which means the viscera are still in the bird and the head and feet are attached. These types of chickens do not appear in U.S. supermarkets these days.*

In Mexico, our value-added product growth has included deboning, tray packing, and offering pre-pricing options for the retailer. We do no cooking of products in Mexico—it's actually more cost-efficient to ship pre-cooked products out of our U.S. operations, rather than remodel Mexico plants for that function.

The Mexico market isn't the same as the U.S. market—and people in international business are wise to recognize that they aren't just exporting an American way of doing things, or an American way of eating, when they move to the international stage.

DIFFERENT DOESN'T MEAN CHEAPER

Some people seem to think that overseas operations can include a lot of cheaper shortcuts, either because the people in the country seem poorer and less savvy to shortcuts, or because the standards of excellence are lower. Neither is true for us!

There are potential perils in doing business in other nations. As just one example, we faced a major problem in 1994 when our earnings dropped 93 percent in one fiscal quarter. What happened? An unexpected devaluation of the Mexican peso! (That same year we had enjoyed record first-quarter sales.)

During the next year, 1995, the peso fell in value by almost 40 percent! Our company profits were depressed by more than $30 million against expectations, and we had a net loss of $7.9 million despite record sales. Even so, Pilgrim's Pride was financially strong and able to withstand the effects of the peso devaluation—and to rebound well. We survived by making our operations in Mexico even more efficient and better positioned.

Maintenance and upgrading of facilities are often more expensive in other nations than in the United States. We have poured a great deal of money into upgrading and renovating our facilities in Mexico through the years. The processing plant at Tepeji del Rio is one of three very sophisticated operations we have there now. It produces about 1.1 million chickens a week in a plant that is near the huge Mexico City metropolitan area. To reach such a high level of production, we needed to add two ice plants, a mechanical workshop for the truck fleet, and a waiting area for live-haul and processed-chicken vehicles.

At the San Luis Potosi operation, we tripled capacity, which meant adding an eighty-ton ice-making plant and a new well, realigning machinery in the processing plant, and building additional chicken houses in the area. The same was true at Saltillo where the company has a breeder farm, chicken houses, a hatchery, a feed mill, and a processing plant.

Our main market in Mexico is Mexico City, of course. The city has a population that exceeds 22 million people at present count. We have a multistory office building in Mexico City where more than sixty Pilgrim's Partners work in sales, human resources, marketing, credit, and collections.

Our headquarters in Mexico are actually in Queretaro, where the company has two feed mills, five hatcheries, and 1,334 chicken houses. Our processing plants and feed mills are all modern facilities. In fact, when modernizing the feed mill we added a system capable of handling shuttle trains with 110 cars.

I am very proud of—and am very committed to maintaining—the high quality of our operations in Mexico. The facilities are comparable to those we have in the United States, and our employees in Mexico are competent, committed, and just as proud to be part of the Pilgrim's Pride team as those in the United States.

We own 44.5 percent of our chicken-house capacity in Mexico, and we have U.S.-style contracts with the other 55.5 percent. We grow about 3.7 million birds a week in Mexico, and our live operations include feed milling. The breeder pullet production is on large, beautiful, relatively isolated farms, which are all company owned. We have two large breeder farms in the state of Coahuila, each with forty-eight houses equipped with the most modern technology. Our other two breeder farms are in the state of Queretaro.

I refer to our operations there as our "mile-high" chickens. Most of our poultry production facilities are at an altitude of 5,800 feet above sea level.

Even with added expenses and monetary fluctuations, the future seems very bright to us in Mexico. Poultry consumption in that nation is growing at a more rapid pace than in the United States. The market has more than 100 million consumers. And we consistently are rated in the top third of all chicken companies in all phases of customer satisfaction and overall performance.

We are the number two poultry company in Mexico in terms of volume, and we continue to grow.

¡Viva México!

★ ★ ★

All the law is fulfilled in one word, even in this: "You shall love your neighbor as yourself." But if you bite and devour one another, beware lest you be consumed by one another!
(Gal. 5:14–15 NKJV)

12

Riding the Unpredictable Waves of the Poultry Industry

Agribusiness—and farming in general—is one of the trickiest businesses any person can pursue. So many of the variables that can produce a make-or-break year are simply beyond the control of human beings. I learned very early in this business that bankers and investors aren't very fond of unpredictability.

Neither is Wall Street. It doesn't matter that Pilgrim's Pride was first named to the Fortune 500 in 1989. Wall Street has never particularly liked the idea of investing in companies where the prices fluctuate, sometimes wildly, and whose futures depend in large measure on factors that are beyond a corporate executive's control. Nevertheless, that's the nature of the poultry industry!

I have spent only one sleepless night in my life—it was the night my brother Aubrey died in April of 1966. Aubrey and I were brothers and business partners. Nobody was closer to me. The night he died I spent hours tossing and turning, wondering what would happen to me . . . to the business . . . to our customers . . . to our lenders . . . to our employees. It was a night filled with worry. I played and replayed countless scenarios of what might happen and what might become of us all. It was also a night of doubt. I wondered if I could operate the company on my own— if I had what it took to be the chief executive officer and to take on the tasks that Aubrey had been doing.

Near morning I made a decision: "I am going to run this company."

That single decision gave my life direction from that day forward. It is a decision that is still in effect. I took full responsibility for making Pilgrim's Pride a spectacular success story. I boldly took the reins of leadership. I had every hope and intention and motivating desire to run the company to even greater heights. Failure was not an option.

I believe such a decision is critical to the success of any person, especially to the leader of any organization or company. A leader who is coaxed into leadership rarely turns out to be much of a leader. A leader who boldly takes on the mantle of leadership at least has a shot at becoming great.

The next three years were not easy ones—in fact, the phrase to describe them might be "extremely tumultuous."

First, we seemed to struggle a little to find our right corporate identity and definition. We changed the company name three times—from Pilgrim Feed Mill to Pilgrim's Corporation in October 1969, to Pilgrim Industries, Inc., just two months later in December 1969. That was our name until June 27, 1985, when the name Pilgrim's Pride Corporation was adopted.

Second, we experienced tremendous growth.

The feed mill's capacity was tripled. We spent $175,000 to add a 150-horsepower pellet mill, a three-ton bulk hopper scale, and two sections of storage bins to enlarge the mill's capacity to 2,400 tons a week. As part of the expansion, we became a molasses broker. We initially purchased molasses—a feed additive—from a company in Houston for our own feed mixes, but we then began selling molasses in large quantities to fifteen other feed mills.

We were producing 300,000 baby chicks by the end of the decade, the full capacity of our hatchery, and we also began processing and marketing commercial eggs under the name "Pilgrim's Pride."

Third, we faced what could have been major financial problems.

When I think back on that time, it seems as if I spent a great deal of my time and energy working on financial deals to allow for our rapid expansion.

Much of our growth and success to that point had been possible because the financial community repeatedly provided the funds we needed for day-to-day operations or for major expansions. In 1969, we were doing financial business primarily with CIT Corporation, and we were able to reach an agreement with Associates Finance of North America to make operating funds available through a plan that involved refinancing the feed mill. After years of trying to work out a deal, we were also able to secure funds for financing live chickens from the Production Credit Association of Nashville, Arkansas. The Nashville PCA was successful in getting permission from the Federal Intermediate Credit Bank of St. Louis to extend credit arrangements into Northeast Texas. With these new financial arrangements, the poultry business was not only growing rapidly throughout Arkansas, but also moving into Northeast Texas through Pilgrim's.

When Marshall Credit Production Association merged with the Crockett, Texas, operations, Pilgrim's Pride was able to get a waiver from Crockett headquarters because their expertise was primarily in cotton and cattle. The Crockett officials had little experience in financing poultry. Nashville PCA was then able to put together additional help from the Red River Production Credit Association and the Pine Bluff, Arkansas, Credit Association to offer, ultimately, a sizable operating line of credit for our inventory as well as financing for other facilities that we needed as we grew.

We used some of this extended credit to help Sam Hatcher and Jack Miller establish a second processing plant in Mount Pleasant. This partnership had secured a Small Business Administration loan to finance the plant but required more funds and chickens to get the plant operating profitably. I agreed to supply what they needed in return for a one-third interest in the Golden Feast Poultry Processing Plant. We later acquired a 50 percent interest in this company, and even later we owned 100 percent and merged it into Pilgrim's Pride.

RIDING THE MARKETS INTO THE SEVENTIES

Understanding the chicken market is very simple: for every chicken you can't sell, you lose money. For every chicken you sell for less than what it costs you to hatch and raise the chicken, you lose money. No producer wants to have more chickens available for sale than the marketplace wants to purchase. No producer can survive selling at a loss, at least not for very long.

The early years of the 1970s were a particularly bad time for the chicken business. The government imposed a retail price freeze in 1973 for sixty days at a time when wholesale feed costs were soaring and growers were destroying chicks rather than feed them for two months and sell them at a loss. A competitor was reported in the *Wall Street Journal* (July 15, 1974) as drowning 300,000 chicks and destroying 800,000 eggs as it phased out a facility until chicken production became profitable again. Another farmer reportedly gave away about 2,200 laying hens rather than accept a price of four cents a pound for them at market. These dramatic actions were not unusual.

In response to these market conditions, poultry producers created the National Broiler Marketing Association (NBMA) under the auspices of the Capper-Volstead Act that allowed cooperative marketing in agriculture industries. I was part of the group that created this organization. Prices immediately began to rise for chickens, and for several years, poultry producers finally earned a profit.

This group shared price information among its members—as allowed under federal law. Our membership represented about 70 percent of the market share in the broiler industry. Later, the Justice Department sued the NBMA, stating that broker producers were operating counter to antitrust legislation. The issue went to the Supreme Court, and in the end, major producers were fined hundreds of thousands of dollars. By that time, however, the price freeze had been lifted, and most of these companies were on more solid financial footing again.

The chicken business from the 1970s into the 1980s had many ups and downs. A number of the downs related to government regulations that always seemed to be shifting. For example, federal tax laws in the 1970s allowed chicken operations to use cash accounting rather than accrual accounting. With cash accounting, a company might book sales when a check arrived from a customer, and then book expenses when a check was written to a vendor. This meant that toward the end of a profitable year a company might buy additional feed for the following year, write a check for it, and take that expense immediately. Then in 1989, the government eliminated cash accounting for large companies.

Our industry is an industry of "pennies and grams." If we can reduce our costs by just one penny per dollar and increase our sales by just one penny per dollar, we improve our bottom line 2 percent! That's basic math, of course, but the principle should never be forgotten.

Situations such as these simply compound what is the basic reality for the poultry business: Raising chickens is unpredictable, financially speaking. Just the smallest change in soy meal and corn prices, or a one or two cent per-pound change in the sale price of chicken, can have a great effect on a poultry company.

I have often said that our industry is an industry of "pennies and grams." If we can reduce our costs by just one penny per dollar and increase our sales by just one penny per dollar, we improve our bottom line 2 percent! That's basic math, of course, but the principle should never be forgotten.

We don't create a product that sells for thousands of dollars. We create a product that is sold by the pound—and generally speaking, the price per pound is a few dollars and cents.

An interesting thing about this is that a customer generally makes a buying decision about fresh chicken based on the cost of a package of chicken rather than the cost per pound. We need to stay on top of the package cost, not just the per-pound cost, that is acceptable to a retail customer.

BIG-MONEY FLUCTUATIONS

The cost of producing chickens, and the price we receive for the amount we produce, can fluctuate millions of dollars a year. These are mind-boggling figures to me.

The change in the price of stock can also be mind-boggling.

Pilgrim's Pride Corporation went public on the New York Stock Exchange on November 15, 1986, under the symbol CHX. More than $50 million in stock was sold as a major step toward financing expansions. We used the money to purchase the interests of Doris Julian (Aubrey Pilgrim's widow) and her three children. As a result of this buyout, I became owner of 80 percent of the company.

My ownership was later restructured so that today I own about 38 percent of the company and am the largest shareholder. I watch the price of Pilgrim's Pride stock as closely as anybody! If I didn't know my own company, there might be times when the fluctuations in stock could become discouraging. The good news is that I do know my own company, and therefore, I am extremely encouraged the vast majority of the time.

Fluctuations in the poultry business can be so extreme that any profits are wiped out in any given quarter or year. The normal fluctuation in cost of production can be two to four cents a pound in any given quarter;

that translates into $120 to 250 million a year at the volume we produce. Most of this fluctuation is due to the cost of corn and soybean meal.

The selling price can also fluctuate $120 to 250 million a year. This depends in part on how many chickens are being produced, not only by us but by our competitors.

Certainly we do everything we can to manage these fluctuations, so that our costs and selling prices don't fluctuate drastically. The size of the company drives all four of these figures (production costs, selling prices, profit, and stock price). Everything must be kept in a very careful balance for a solid profit to emerge.

One day in 2004, we experienced an extreme and unprecedented drop in our stock value. For me personally, the one-day loss represented more than $81 million. A friend asked me how I felt at seeing that loss appear in the daily financial report I receive from my financial executives. I responded, "All is well. Praise the Lord!"

The truth is, I don't let a fluctuation like this influence me. I knew that Pilgrim's Pride was sound in every measurable way. I had an even greater confidence that the Lord is in charge of my life and, through me, my business. I have been through these fluctuations for so many years that I also have confidence that what goes down will eventually go up—the fluctuations are cyclical. Sure enough, within a few months, the value of our stock had been restored.

One day in 2004, we experienced an extreme and unprecedented drop in our stock value. For me personally, the one-day loss represented more than $81 million. A friend asked me how I felt at seeing that loss appear in the daily financial report. I responded, "All is well. Praise the Lord!"

What these fluctuations mean from a business standpoint is that we face a special need in working with knowledgeable lending organizations that understand the volatility and demanding needs of a company such as ours.

Rapid Growth Can Mean
Rapid Debt Growth

I've come to realize over the years that with rapid growth one can easily experience rapid debt growth!

One of the major challenges we have faced as a corporation was a restructuring of our debt and finances through a $100 million public bond offering in 1993. As part of that restructuring effort, Cliff Butler, our chief financial officer at the time, Lindy M. "Buddy" Pilgrim, who had assumed the reins as president of Pilgrim's Pride, and I headed out for a two-week coast-to-coast "road show" with Donaldson, Lufkin & Jenrette Securities Corp. At one point we covered twelve major financial-center cities in the United States, as well as cities in two foreign nations, in an eight-day period. We called on more than forty major bond investors in our effort to market the bonds. We were successful.

The offering restructured much of our debt, including lowering interest rates and extending maturities. We also secured a new group of six banks to provide a $75 million line of operating capital. Our operations results were strong, and the new financing positioned us to take on the future.

Why share stories such as these?

Because anybody who is entering the poultry industry—or any aspect of agribusiness—needs to have a special dose of courage.

The story of Fieldale Farms, a long-standing and major poultry producer in the past, has been documented in a book. One line in the introduction of that book caught my attention: "It takes a particular brand of guts to run a poultry company." I couldn't agree more.

The key to surviving in today's business world without losing sleep—or acquiring ulcers—is to have faith in your product, faith in your company, and most important, faith in the Lord. I don't know how people make it who don't have faith in God. He's the One who makes the waves, and He's the One who calms them. On a day-to-day basis, He's also the One who gives us the ability to ride the waves without capsizing personally or corporately.

★   ★   ★

God has dealt to each one a measure of faith.
(Rom. 12:3 NKJV)

13

To Acquire
or Be Acquired—
That Is Very Often
the Challenge!

In 1969, while attending a business seminar, I learned an invaluable lesson about mergers and acquisitions.

Several Harvard professors were teaching this seminar that explained discounted cash flow and the present value of money. They proposed that a person could go out and find someone who wanted to sell a business, use cash, and reach an agreement to pay over an extended period of time. That was a new idea to me, but I quickly caught on to its merit! Pilgrim's Pride moved into a period of growth by acquisition, which became something of a hallmark for the entire next decade.

We first acquired Market Produce Company of Fort Worth, which had facilities in Arlington, Corsicana, Odessa, and El Paso, Texas. We paid $2.1 million for this company and used its cash to pay Arch Myrick for his company over a long term.

We purchased a Mount Pleasant canning plant from John B. Stevens, and in 1971 we began to pack individually quick frozen (IQF) cooked and fresh chicken there. We were ten to fifteen years ahead of our time, and the production line was soon discontinued. Today, however, IQF is a significant part of our income. We also purchased two other plants from Stephens: the NE Texas Packing Co. and a rendering plant in Mount

Pleasant. The facilities did not have room for growth and needed modernization. We eventually tore down the structures and built a new state-of-the-art protein conversion plant in 1975. The plant has been upgraded a number of times through the years. It can render beef products as well as poultry offal. The by-products from this plant become pet food ingredients that are sold to large companies such as Ralston Purina, Kal-Can, Carnation, and Iams.

We purchased the Graham Feed Elevator in Rosser, Texas, which had a capacity of 300,000 bushels of grain. It supplemented our Pittsburg storage facilities.

In 1974 we leased a poultry processing plant in Dallas and later purchased it.

We opened our second hatchery—which we rather uncreatively called Hatchery No. 2—in 1975 and set ourselves a goal of producing 1 million chickens a week by September 1979. We reached that goal.

Not all of our expansion plans and acquisitions went well. Our main failure came far from home—out in California.

We were hoping to move into the fast-food industry and retail supermarkets in Los Angeles with the purchase of the Crenshaw Foods Corporation in December 1975. This company had been a distributor of poultry, beef, pork, fish, and many other items in the Southern California area. It was in bankruptcy, and we made the purchase from the bankruptcy judge with the understanding that the business would not be closed during the bankruptcy proceedings. Later the judge thought it was necessary to close the business to get an accurate accounting of the inventory, and in so doing, all of the established business was lost. Customers lost confidence in future deliveries, and we struggled for more than two years to salvage the business and regain their confidence, but failed. We eventually had to close that operation because we simply were losing too much money. We sold the property to Tropicana Orange Juice of Florida.

Breaking into
the Top Ten

We purchased Mountaire Poultry Company of De Queen and Nashville, Arkansas, in September 1981. This company was about one-third the size of Pilgrim's. The acquisition gave us national recognition and made our company one of the top ten chicken producers in the United States.

Included in this purchase were a processing plant and hatchery in De Queen, and a hatchery and feed mill in Nashville. Prior to our acquisition of Mountaire, all of our Pilgrim's products were sold in bulk to customers, including supermarkets and chain restaurants. The purchase of the De Queen facility provided the opportunity to enter the retail prepackaged chicken business (chill pack) in 1983.

To accompany the new chill-pack processing capabilities in De Queen, the company opened a new sales and marketing headquarters in Dallas in January 1983. All sales and marketing responsibilities were consolidated under this centralized group. It was the beginning of our making a major marketing effort—and this, in turn, moved us beyond bulk commodity sales.

A man who joined our company through the Mountaire acquisition was Bob Hendrix, someone who continues to be a great contributor to this day. Several years later at a management meeting in Dallas, I presented Bob with a unique award. I told the group that I was so proud of the job Bob was doing that I was willing to give him the shirt off my back. It dawned on me that I should put action to my words! So, I unbuttoned my shirt, took it off, and gave it to him. He still has it.

Not all of the business I did was conducted through the company, however. As an example, in 1981, I personally purchased 50 percent interest in Golden Feast, which was owned by Lane Poultry Company. Two years later, I sold this operation to Pilgrim Industries, Inc., and we discontinued the Golden Feast name and gave our own name to the products.

In May 1982 we bought the Strube Egg Farms, which produced 2.4 million laying hens for the production of table eggs.

Our Brief Negotiations with Tyson

In 1988, I found myself facing an unusual convergence of financial situations, and the net effect of them was that we began losing a considerable amount of money—approximately $1 million a week!

That's a lot of money to be losing, and I knew that if things didn't turn around, we'd crash on the rocks of bankruptcy within a few months. I offered to sell the company to Tyson Foods for about nine dollars a share. We negotiated a letter of intent, but seven days later, Tyson Foods abruptly made a decision not to close the deal.

As we were discussing this situation, a member of our board made a very simple statement to me: "Bo, the Lord has given your company back to you." That really hit me. I knew it was the truth. I went home from that meeting and read through every passage I could find in the Bible that dealt with the promises of God.

> A member of our board made a very simple statement to me: "Bo, the Lord has given your company back to you." That really hit me. I knew it was the truth. I went home from that meeting and read through every passage I could find in the Bible that dealt with the promises of God.

I made a decision that night that was as important as the decision I made to run the company in 1966 after Aubrey died. This time it was a decision that we would continue to run the company, and more important, that we would put our full trust in the Lord to bring us through this difficult time and that we would believe Him for a successful turnaround.

The next day I announced to the board that we were going to continue operating and that we would trust God for a miracle.

Within five months, things had turned around so that we were making $1 million a week instead of losing that much money. We went forward with a $50 million, 14.5 percent public bond offering through First Boston Corporation.

As part of our turnaround effort, we thought that perhaps we should bring in new management personnel. We thought wrong. That proved to be a major mistake on our part, one we corrected as quickly as possible.

The truth is, most of our day-to-day successes and our major achievements have resulted from the work of management and hourly personnel—people we genuinely call "Partners"—who have been with the company for many years and have dedication and loyalty that can't easily be found on the outside.

During the time that we took in the new management personnel, we were growing rapidly, but as is often the case, with rapid growth can come rapid growth of debt. We had spent more than $100 million in Mexico. We arranged for a $50 million loan but overspent the loan covenant. And at the same time, we suddenly began to lose money rapidly in Mexico and in the United States. Some creditors were very unhappy with the heavy investments in Mexico, and they blocked the closing of the loan covenant. We parted ways with the new management personnel in August 1992, and the next month, we faced our worst fiscal year ever with an after-tax loss of $29.7 million. The loss, combined with the Mexico expansion, not only made some of our creditors very unhappy, but some of them began to challenge the company's judgment and to withdraw financing. The lenders also wanted to force the company to sell our Mexico investments.

I refused to do that. We countered by selling $30 million worth of previously unissued stock to Archer Daniels Midland Company. This new infusion of equity offset the 1992 losses and demonstrated our commitment to the company and my personal confidence that the people of Pilgrim's Pride, under new leadership, could turn the situation around.

Morale soared. A phenomenal financial turnaround began late in the calendar year 1992, and we fully restored our financial structure in early 1993.

In 1997, we acquired Green Acre Foods in Southeast Texas, and a large further-processing plant nearby in Waco, Texas, two years later.

TAKING ON TURKEYS

One challenge often encountered in an acquisition is adding a new product that has not been produced by the parent company, or perhaps adding a product that has not been emphasized by the parent company. We experienced such a challenge in our acquisition of WLR Foods. That acquisition put us back in the turkey business in a major way. We had been in the turkey business in earlier years—mostly unsuccessfully. All things considered, turkeys are a tough business.

Every industry or business likely has one area in which the corporate executives see far more potential for a product than the customers see. From my perspective, that area is turkey.

Turkeys are big, grand birds. Just watching them strut around a poultry pen makes a person smile. The economics of turkey growing and turkey processing, however, can sometimes give a poultry executive a major headache.

For one thing, turkeys are tied closely to one major holiday meal, Thanksgiving, and secondarily to Christmas. That means a lot of turkeys need to be available in a very short period of time—usually in the space of a month. The rest of the year, selling turkeys is a challenge.

It isn't that turkey is any less versatile, less nutritious, or less tasty than chicken. It has just as much protein and is a great dollar value per pound. The processing of turkeys is not all that different from the processing of chickens.

The difference lies in public perception of what turkey is. It's been a very slow consumer education process over the last several decades to convince people that a barbecued turkey makes a great Fourth of July dinner, that turkey can be marinated and grilled, that turkey sausage and turkey patties are great substitutes for pork and beef products.

In some circles, turkey is making progress—but it's almost as if turkey has to sneak into the kitchen. One person told me recently that she mixes freshly ground turkey breast from her supermarket into lean ground beef in equal portions and uses the mix in everything that she used to make with only ground beef: patties, meatloaf, chili, meatballs, and meat sauces. She said, "The result is just as tasty, much lower in fat, and more economical." That was music to my ears!

Today, our turkey business is focused on value-added products, including our Signature line of premium turkeys that are basted with real butter.

THE ACQUISITION OF CONAGRA POULTRY— OUR LARGEST DEAL

As I mentioned in the opening of this book, we acquired ConAgra's chicken division in 2003—the largest acquisition ever in the poultry industry. Many people were surprised at this acquisition because the deal was so big, and because we had just acquired WLR Foods in 2001.

What did we consider in making this acquisition?

First, the ConAgra operation was a quality operation.

Second, we had good experiences with previous acquisitions.

Third, the move was in keeping with our corporate strategic objectives, which I shared in an earlier chapter:

- Be the preferred supplier to our customers.
- Grow at twice the industry rate.
- Be in the top 25 percent in efficiencies in all processes and services.

- Consistently earn net profit of 4 percent or more to create value for our shareholders.
- Be a great place to work!

We are a business, and I make no apologies for making money. That's what a business does, first and foremost. We have set a goal of a 4 percent profit margin. That allows us to treat our Partners and our shareholders right.

To be profitable now and in the years ahead, we need to be a leader in our industry. I make no apology for wanting to outperform our competitors. That's what a successful business does. I am all for playing hard and playing fair.

In order to stay in a leadership position, we need to be a leader not only in the overall big picture but in specific segments of the market. In our company, these seven segments are ones in which we intend to be a leader: retail, foodservice, industrial, national accounts, export of chicken, eggs, and turkey.

SEEKING TO ENHANCE

The net effect of our acquiring the ConAgra Poultry division was that overnight we doubled our size. The best part of this acquisition, however, was not the growth in volume, but the fact that we felt we had made an acquisition that gave us greater flexibility and strength for future growth and adaptation to market changes—without any change in our essential nature. ConAgra didn't alter who we were or are. That division of ConAgra only emphasized and enhanced our basic characteristics as a corporation. ConAgra brands—such as Pierce®, Easy Entrees®, and Country Pride®—blended well with our brands.

We knew that we would be able to build our customer base without any sacrifice in customer service commitment, and that we would be in a position to seek new customer relationships that would be healthy and beneficial on a win-win basis.

We also knew that we had a tremendous opportunity to market our brands nationally, not just regionally.

In some ways, ConAgra enhanced our capacity—we are better able to provide next-day delivery to 75 percent of the U.S. population and to provide a broader range of products from a single source. There are also ways in which we enhanced what this division of ConAgra was pursuing. The personnel from ConAgra have the satisfaction of knowing upper management is focused on their business—poultry products—because that is our *only* business. There are no distractions. We speak the same business language, support the same research, belong to the same trade associations, and have been affected by the same industry events.

I can't overemphasize these commonalities enough.

In your business—no matter what it is—anytime you seek to acquire another company, to consolidate departments, or to form a good business partnership, I believe these elements need to be in place:

- *You need to go into the new structure with as much financial strength as possible.* We went into the acquisition of ConAgra strong. Our Pilgrim's Pride sales were at $2.6 billion—our seventh consecutive year of growth. Net income grew $42 million over the previous year, resulting in a $1.01 increase in earnings per share.

  One of the adjustments we made just prior to the acquisition of ConAgra was a consolidation of our Class A and Class B stock into a single class of stock. This combination gained approval from the New York Stock Exchange the summer immediately prior to our ConAgra acquisition. All of our stock now trades on the New York Stock Exchange under the symbol PPC.

  I don't mind admitting that I relished the moment when I could ring the opening bell at the New York Stock Exchange on

November 24, 2003, to celebrate the creation of this single class
of stock and our new trading symbol. This move simplified our
capital structure, provided us with an increased liquidity and
trading volume, and gave us greater visibility among investors
and analysts. It also gave us greater flexibility for accessing
capital markets or issuing additional stock in the future.

- *You must be able to speak the same business language.* Growout is
not a term for hand-me-down clothing or a hairstyle. People in
the chicken business know that. Other people often don't.

  A great deal of time and energy can be spent learning a
language if you aren't already using the same jargon and have the
same meanings for terms.

- *You must support the same research.* Ultimately both need to build
on the same foundation of facts and principles. If your R & D
teams have a different understanding of what is good, accurate,
or beneficial, you're in trouble.

- *You must belong to the same trade associations.* This is where
information is exchanged and vital relationships are built for
mutual support. If you are moving in different spheres, you are
not going to emerge as a strong unit.

- *You need to have a similar history—having been affected by similar
events in your industry.* There's a tremendous shorthand if both
have been through some of the same experiences, grappled with
some of the same issues, and supported some of the same causes.

In fact, the more I reflect on this, I can see how these basics apply to
just about any form of organization or mutually beneficial partnership a
person might create. They certainly apply to a person who moves into a
community and seeks a church to join. It helps if you speak the language,
have the same understanding of truth, know some of the key people and
have some relationships in common (especially your relationship with

Jesus Christ), and have a similar outlook on the world's problems and the solutions a church might offer to them.

It's also true for a marriage. One of the things that has been of tremendous value in my marriage relationship with Patty is that we come from the same roots. She's from Camp County. Although she is about ten years younger than I, we grew up in the same area, know the same landmarks, and have known many of the same people all of our lives. We share the same values and core beliefs. We speak the same language . . . East Texan!

There's one more factor that's important in an acquisition or merger. Somebody needs to lead—somebody needs to be in charge. Pilgrim's Pride acquired ConAgra's chicken division. Pilgrim's Pride leads. That's also true in other forms of relationships. A leaderless group goes nowhere fast.

> *Compromise is not wise if both parties give up something that makes each party weaker in the end, just for the sake of some form of agreement. Seek a higher good; set a better goal; pursue a loftier mission; go after a greater benefit.*

There are always adjustments in an acquisition or a merger of any type. I don't want to underplay the need for being willing to make adjustments and some compromises when it comes to the way things are done. My approach to compromise is this: compromise only if the end result makes both of you stronger. Compromise is not wise if both parties give up something that makes each party weaker in the end, just for the sake of some form of agreement. Seek a higher good; set a better goal; pursue a loftier mission; go after a greater benefit.

Although we've had our share of adjustments with ConAgra, thus far, we've found the experience very positive. We've learned a lot from each other, especially in customer service, purchasing, production, and transportation. I personally have enjoyed the process. It's fun making new friends who have similar interests and goals. We both are looking to grow and become better—and that's a wonderful core concept to keep in mind in any joining together of forces!

★   ★   ★

Come now, you who say, "Today or tomorrow we will go
to such and such a city, spend a year there, buy and sell,
and make a profit." . . . Instead you ought to say,
"If the Lord wills, we shall live and do this or that."
(James 4:13, 15 NKJV)

14

MARKS OF A SUCCESSFUL CEO

I learned to shoot in the military, but unlike many men in East Texas, I wasn't much into hunting. Then one day some men invited me to go on a deer hunting trip, and to my surprise—and their shock—I dropped a buck with one shot from 280 yards. The bullet went straight through the buck's heart.

It's a chief executive officer's responsibility to go straight for the bull's-eye when it comes to making decisions and running a company. Anything other than the bull's-eye is going to affect the bottom line.

From time to time I've been asked to speak to various groups on leadership. If there's a formula for success in business, I think it's probably this:

$$(Education + Skills) \times Motivation = Results$$

This formula applies to the success of an individual executive and also to a team of people in a company. For our purposes in this chapter, we'll focus on you as a leader.

EDUCATION

What you know includes your inherited intelligence—your ability to reason and think logically. It includes formal schooling and the information you've acquired through the years by means of experience and personal study. Education is always gained by some effort on a person's part—it isn't just "hearing" something. It's paying close attention to what is heard. It's remembering and using information. It's learning from mistakes and not making the same mistake twice. A person needs to get all the education he or she needs in order to do what is necessary for reaching a goal.

SKILLS

People are born with an ability to do something—everybody has at least one inborn skill or talent. Skills need to be developed. Over time, many skills are developed on the basis of life experience or on-the-job experience. A person needs to develop his or her skills to the highest level possible.

An important skill to develop is your memory. I've been blessed with a good memory. Some people think it's a photographic memory. I do seem to remember things that are visual—including names or words that I see written down. No matter how good or poor your memory, do your best to improve it. It's important that you remember what you've promised, the deals you've made, the names of your customers and key information about them, the experiences that go into decisions you make, and previous problems that you've solved.

MOTIVATION

This is drive, "fire in the belly," a move toward action. It includes an ability to take the initiative, focus on goals, and be self-directed. It is a mindset aimed at solving problems or acquiring things that are desired. Motivation isn't a sporadic burst of energy. It's a lifestyle of seeking to do more, be more, and accomplish more.

Nobody can or will ever motivate you like you'll motivate yourself.

And unless you motivate yourself, you won't seek to develop your intelligence or skills. You won't desire to pursue greater goals.

RESULTS

Results is another word for desired outcome—which may be wealth, power or success. It is achievement.

FOCUS ON THE ASPECTS OF YOUR BUSINESS THAT ARE LIVING

Beyond the formula I've described, I believe it is very important for a top executive to focus primarily on the aspects of the business that are alive. The growth of any business is directly related to what can grow, and what can grow are things that are alive. People can grow. Skills and ideas can grow because they are resident in people who can grow. Teams can grow. It is because people grow that productivity grows, efficiency increases, and quality improves.

Chickens are alive, and it's wonderful if you have a product that is alive. There's great potential for growth!

As I noted earlier in this book, chicken consumption has been growing at a rate hovering around 6 percent per year. That means chicken-producing companies need to be growing at something of a similar rate, especially if they want to remain a major player in the industry.

More chicken consumption means the need for more chickens—which in turn means the need not only for more hatcheries but more chicken houses, as well as the need for more feed production and more processing capacity.

If one part of the company grows, all parts of the company need to keep pace.

In every industry I know, growth at a 6 percent pace is a challenge, but it's a special challenge when you are dealing with a living product that is subject to all sorts of factors. By living products I'm referring not only to the chickens and other farm animals we handle, but also to the various grains and substances that comprise the feed used in our formulations. Not only does the growth need to be coordinated in all areas, but it needs to be done with the greatest amount of efficiency in transportation from one segment of the operation to the next.

Living entities, of course, are subject to factors that can inhibit growth or even cause death. This is true not only for chickens, but also for feed grains. Growth is possible only if all systems are functioning and healthy.

All things considered, agribusiness—and in our specific case, the chicken business—represents a challenge that is likely to keep even a highly experienced executive on his or her toes. This business certainly causes me to get up every morning with a high degree of enthusiasm and expectancy. Why? Because I'm dealing with a living, breathing, moving, and growing entity!

STAY FOCUSED ON SOLUTIONS

Susan Combs is the commissioner of agriculture for the state of Texas. She likes to tell a story about her first day in her new office. She walked into her office and noticed something on top of the bookcase. Susan is six feet two inches tall so she reached up to see if she could pull down the object she could barely see. It turned out to be a stuffed chicken, about eighteen inches tall, standing on a pedestal at the back of the bookshelf. I had given it to her predecessor, Rick Perry. Susan says, "I laughed when I read the plaque at the base of that chicken. It said, 'The Answer to Mad Cow Disease.' That was my introduction to Bo Pilgrim. I'll never forget it."

I'm a man who likes to come up with solutions to problems, and I tend to stay focused on solutions.

Most people are content with the way their lives are. Oh, they may complain about things, but they are never really discontented enough to make any changes. For years statisticians have told us that only about 1 percent of the population reaches the top of anything—career, company leadership, physical fitness, education, or any other arena of life. About 4 percent will reach what is called the "leadership level." The rest will plateau someplace lower than leadership.

What makes the difference between the 5 percent who achieve lofty success and the 95 percent who don't? Very often it's this: 95 percent keep their eyes focused on problems and obstacles. The 5 percent keep their eyes focused on solutions and goals.

Take on Problems One at a Time

Sometimes you can solve two or more problems with one solution, but generally speaking, every problem has its own solution. That means each problem needs to be tackled as a unique entity. Take on one problem at a time.

The growth of most companies—for that matter, the growth of any one sector of a company—can be viewed as a sequence of problems that were solved one at a time, over time.

Many young people seem to think that people who have stories like mine have taken some sort of dramatic leap from having nothing to having everything. They read the headline, "From One Feed Store to a $5 Billion Corporation," and they think the road was easy, with plenty of time for leisure pursuits and personal pleasure.

I don't know any successful person today who has built a company from nothing and has done it either quickly or easily.

Every day for decades has been filled with small problems—some of them slightly less small than others, some of them trickier to solve than others, some of them more persistent than others.

Building something great is never easy.

Building something excellent is never a foregone conclusion, even with the best efforts.

There's always something that can break, some person who can disappoint, some backstage politicking that seems to be taking place, some process that doesn't live up to its theory, some customer who makes a decision totally beyond your ability to control it, and very likely somebody who dislikes you or is jealous of you, even though you attempt to be as likable and generous as possible.

That's just the way life and business are.

Nobody wins *all* the time.

What's important in the end is that you don't lose all the time! And what's even more important is that you know deep down inside that your motives have been good, your character remains intact, and your trust in the Lord is strong. God can turn things around that no person can turn around—He has ways and means that are higher and greater than anything a person can conceive.

> Nobody wins all the time. What's important in the end is that you don't lose all the time! And what's even more important is that you know deep down inside that your motives have been good, your character remains intact, and your trust in the Lord is strong.

The political process is nearly always involved to some degree when a person is solving problems. Sometimes the political process *is* the problem. I have never worn rose-colored glasses when it comes to understanding small-town politics. Politics in smaller towns can be intense—just as volatile as politics in big cities and at higher levels of government.

When we proposed expansion of our flagship poultry-processing facility in Mount Pleasant, opposition against the idea was expressed almost immediately. The owner of a furniture business and a former mayor organized Northeast Texans for a Better Tomorrow. This man claimed to be all in favor of the "local poultry business"—namely, us—but he opposed our plans to double the facility already in place.

The mayor of Mount Pleasant, Bill Chambers, tried to bring both sides together, and I was more than happy to sit down at a table to discuss what we wanted to do and why. I certainly was motivated by a desire to expand the business *and* to be a force for good in Mount Pleasant. In the end, the man opposing us also took on the mayor and opposed him in the next election.

At that point, rather than fuel a community fight any further, I withdrew our plans. We turned to a different plan—one that we felt was an even *better* plan. We decided to acquire existing facilities rather than build new ones. And this decision led to the acquisition of ConAgra's chicken division.

If one thing doesn't work out as you hoped, that isn't a signal to give up. It's a signal to come up with something better.

Stay Focused on Getting and Keeping Customers

Chickens don't really propel our business toward the future. Our customers propel us forward. They express to us the ideas and needs that generate new products. They give us the orders that grow our business and cause us to expand in various areas. Customer care is vital, and an abiding concern for customers needs to flow from the very top of an organization.

Through the years, many people in the business world have been surprised that we chose a statement from the Bible as our Guiding Principle: "However you want people to treat you, so treat them" (see Matt. 7:12). This statement is at the heart of customer service. We believe strongly that our job is to provide outstanding customer satisfaction every day.

We don't have just one customer, of course. We have the grocery shopper who is looking for a nutritious meal that he or she can take home, heat up, and eat in the space of fifteen minutes. We have the grocery shopper who actually cooks—who wants high-quality fresh chicken and eggs.

We also have the buyer for the grocery store who wants the best product for the cheapest price, the receiving agent who needs timely delivery, and the meat market manager who wants neat, clean packages for display.

We also have many other customers, including restaurants, quick-service chain restaurants, and food-service distributors.

So, we have to satisfy a wide variety of people—with different needs—on any given day.

Pursue the Accounts You Want— with Persistence!

Every account is worth pursuing and, once gained, worth keeping. I worked hard years ago to get some of the accounts that we still have today. I was persistent in pursuing the customers I wanted.

Sonny Williams, who was then president and chief operating officer of Minyard Food Stores, Inc., recently told a mutual friend how he first met me thirty years ago. He said, "Bo just showed up in the lobby of our corporate headquarters at Minyard Food Stores, Inc., in Dallas and asked to meet with me. He was polite, but persistent. He showed up without an appointment dressed in a solid white suit and hat, and wanted to sit down with me and ask Minyard Food Stores for our chicken business. At the time, our chain of stores was selling another brand and not offering Pilgrim's Pride. I listened to Bo's proposal and told him we were happy with the poultry company we were currently doing business with, but I told him I would think about his proposal and give him a call back. Bo thanked me for listening and left the meeting.

"Two weeks later I unexpectedly got another call from our lobby receptionist saying that Bo Pilgrim was back, without an appointment, asking to speak with me. Again, he was wearing his solid white suit and hat. Bo asked me for our chicken business, and again, he reviewed all the reasons why it would be a good move on my part to switch to Pilgrim's Pride. He wouldn't give up. He believed in his product. He wasn't afraid to ask for the order. That was thirty years ago, and we've been in business together ever since."

Believe in your product. If you don't, nobody who works for you will.

Don't be afraid to ask a person for his business. If you are selling a product with high quality at a good price, you are doing him a favor because your product is going to please his customers.

Once you have a person's order, do what you can to help that person resell what you sell to him.

I certainly did that with Minyard Food Stores. For eleven years, Minyard sponsored a three-day-weekend consumer food show at the Dallas Market Hall. It was called the Minyard Food Fest, and usually about 60,000 people attended. There were more than 300 exhibitor booths, daily cooking demonstrations, and musical concerts by top-name recording artists. The Minyard Food Fest became something of a tradition each fall in the Dallas-Fort Worth metroplex. Each year, Pilgrim's Pride had a booth at the show, offered free samples, and gave away cooking recipes and coupons to attendees. For many years I walked the aisles of that show, dressed in my trademark buckled Pilgrim hat with Henrietta the chicken under my arm. The people seemed to enjoy getting an autograph and having their photograph taken with me.

Sonny said to me one time that he thought it was unusual that the CEO of a multimillion-dollar company was walking up and down the aisles of his food show, promoting both Pilgrim's Pride and Minyard Food Stores. I saw it differently—it was an opportunity for me to give a little back to Minyard for the company's believing in us in the early days. That's what corporate friends do.

GIVE THE CUSTOMER
WHAT THE CUSTOMER WANTS

Our customers tell us what to do. How? They tell us what they want—not only the products they desire but the amount they are willing to pay for them. If we listen to our customers closely and accurately, we know what to do with the chickens in our processing plants. It's our salespeople who generally tell us what the customers want. Our R & D Partners take on the technical specifications related to the creation of that product. The operations experts step in to handle manufacturing concerns. Together, these departments select the equipment that does the best job of exceeding customer expectations while still being cost-effective.

Let me give you just a couple of examples about how we responded to our customers' wants.

Grocery store customers told us they wanted 100 percent leak-proof, bead-sealed packaging. They wanted the product fresh and advertised at one price. (Grocery store and meat market managers wanted the same things, for slightly different reasons.)

Grocery store managers also told us they wanted a full line of case-ready products, with category management data to help them improve their efficiency and cost-effectiveness in buying chicken.

We addressed these concerns with a "one weight, one price" line of "Net Weight Case Ready Chicken." The person shopping at the meat counter might not have been consciously aware of this new line when it was introduced, but store managers were! In satisfying our customer's wants, we kept our customers and added new ones.

We rely on our customers to give us valuable information about food trends to help us stay on the cutting edge of our business.

MULTILEVEL CUSTOMER COMMUNICATION

We have never sought mere customers; we have sought people with whom we could have a give-and-take relationship. In many businesses, sales people know buyers. We seek to have strong multifunctional, multilevel relationships and communication with all of our key accounts. In other words, our shipping personnel know the receiving staff on the other end. Our senior management team, R & D team, and quality assurance, processing, marketing, and even accounting personnel are actively engaged with their counterparts in our customers' businesses. The sales managers act more as facilitators, helping us set up a team to coordinate our efforts for a more productive relationship. We don't limit our understanding of productivity to the processing and distribution of items that end up in restaurants and on grocery shelves. We view productivity in terms of people, because people at all levels in our customers' organizations give us the feedback we need to remain a leader in our industry.

LEARN TO MANAGE YOUR TIME VERY WELL

The one thing over which you have total control as an executive is the management of your time. Don't let anybody else force you to keep his or her schedule. Take control of your schedule, and manage your time to meet your goals and agenda.

One of the key decisions I made in my life when it came to time management was a decision about whether I was going to stay on top of all aspects of our corporation, even those in distant locations—and if so, how I was going to manage my travel time.

I made the decision first that I was going to stay very active in meeting with plant managers in the United States, Mexico, and Puerto Rico. I decided I was going to stay in face-to-face contact with key customers as well as with key politicians, lobbyists, and others who were seeking the best for the poultry industry. I decided that I was going to stay in close contact with the public through major public-speaking and public-appearance events.

As we grew, the only way I could effectively manage my time and follow through on these decisions was to take to the air—literally.

For years, I had driven my automobile hundreds of thousands of miles on company business—not only for the acquisitions and the publicity ventures, but also in management of our various enterprises. Increasingly I felt bogged down and limited by the hours that it took to get from East Texas to other locations—the time and effort involved in automobile travel were exhausting.

Getting from zero to an established working product . . . getting from bad to good . . . getting out of the red and into the black . . . that's the hard work. Getting from good to excellent takes just a little more.

We made the move to the air in 1984. Our first twin-engine prop-jet, a Beechcraft Super King Air 300, is still in use today. This plane allowed us to travel for up to six hours non-stop. It seats eight passengers and flies at 365 miles per hour. With the plane I could make a trip to Dallas or De Queen in twenty minutes rather than the two hours these trips often took by car. I could get to Lufkin in twenty-five minutes and Washington, D.C., and Mexico City in less than three hours. We could get to the West Coast in less than five hours. The plane allowed us to "shrink" the geographical area over which I could have personal influence.

In our first plane, I placed a Bible in which I wrote with great sincerity, "Jesus, thank You for the plane." We now have three airplanes, and each of them has a Bible in it. Each of them has a similar inscription.

The fastest trip to New York City we have ever made—with a considerable tailwind—was in our Hawker 800 XP, which we purchased in 2000. We traveled at an average speed of more than 700 miles per hour;

typical speed is 525 miles per hour. It was an amazing ride! Our third plane is also a Hawker 800 XP, which we purchased in 2003.

We have seven pilots and an extra hangar for maintenance. In our transportation department, the aviation department is a department in itself. Not only do we save considerable time, but I'm able to participate in events and meetings that I could not otherwise participate in. It's one of the soundest investments we've made.

NEVER SUBSTITUTE QUALITY

I have a very simple philosophy when it comes to quality. The *best* is the worst I want.

A long-standing friend of mine, Johnny Smith, reminded me recently of something I frequently said to him when we were much younger. In those days people often traded in their car every year or two—if they could afford to do so—and Johnny was always on the lookout for a bargain. He usually bought nice secondhand cars. I usually tried to buy a new car. Johnny said to me, "Bo, I remember how you always used to tell me, 'Smith, it just takes a nickel more to go first class.' I think you were right."

Throughout my life, I've believed that—it takes just a little more to have the best, do your best, and produce the best. Getting from zero to an established working product . . . getting from bad to good . . . getting out of the red and into the black . . . that's the hard work. Getting from good to excellent takes just a little more.

But a little more of what?

A LITTLE FINER INGREDIENTS

In anticipation of Thanksgiving we ran an advertisement for our Pilgrim's Pride turkeys. We put on the wrapper our commitment to going the extra step: "With real butter." We basted our turkeys with real butter so every bite of the bird—dark meat and white meat—would be tender and delicious. We put in a pop-up timer to make turkey preparation easy. And I promised the customer, "If it isn't the best Thanksgiving turkey you've ever served your family, I'll refund your money." To my knowledge, we never had a request for a refund. People wanted the finer ingredient and were willing to pay a little more for it.

A Little More Tender Care

When you have something of quality, take care of it. Value it. Be careful about whom you entrust with its use and maintenance.

When I was drafted into military service, my friends gave me a big going-away party. Each one of the guys there was hoping I'd leave my two-toned blue Pontiac in his care while I was away. I had purchased the car new, and it was a beauty. They were really disappointed when I left the car in the care of my aunt Eva. I wasn't stupid. I knew Aunt Eva would take good care of that car, and it would still be worth driving when I got home!

The Latest in Technology

I don't believe in having the latest in technology just for the sake of saying we have it. I do believe in having the latest in technology if it helps us do a job better, faster, more efficiently, and with less maintenance.

Robots? Yes. We use robotics in several phases of our operation—including robotic water portioners and climate-control devices in chicken houses.

Computers? Absolutely. We use computer-imaging techniques to determine the most efficient use for a piece of meat, and for cutting it precisely using high-speed water jets. We maintain our management information and accounting on huge and complex computing systems.

Latest equipment? Continually. We are always on the search for the state-of-the-art ovens, the most sophisticated new fryers, and the most advanced hatchery equipment. We use new X-ray equipment to analyze boneless meat.

We were at the cutting edge when it came to bar code optical scanning, scale management systems, and corporate information systems. We continually evaluate new retail packaging equipment, just as we continually analyze breed selection.

CONTINUAL MONITORING
FOR QUALITY

We have an outstanding quality assurance department with senior scientists and technicians who study and test everything from food formulas to live production techniques to new plant processes and products. Our quality-assurance technicians conduct more than fifty thousand nutritional and microbiological tests a year to ensure product quality and the greatest operating efficiency.

YOUR NAME ON A PRODUCT REFLECTS YOUR
COMMITMENT TO QUALITY

Do you have a product, a company, or a new business service?

Do you think enough of it to put your name on it?

I do.

My name is Pilgrim, and my company is Pilgrim's Pride. I'm willing to sign my name to every poultry product we produce. I figure that if I can't sign my name to what I produce and what bears my name, then we as a corporation are not producing the quality I want.

There's simply no substitute for quality. My signature is my guarantee of quality. The quality has to go into a product before my name goes on that product.

One of our mind-boggling slogans has been this:

> *The mind-boggling difference in life is*
> *choosing not to be average.*

Through the years, we have won countless "best quality" awards from major customers across the United States. There simply is no substitute for quality. We routinely receive awards that have these words or phrases in them:

- Preferred
- Partners

- Leader
- Top 10
- Excellent

- No. 1
- Quality

These words and phrases describe what it means to be a world-class food company.

Pilgrim's Pride was named one of the "Most Admired Companies in America" by *Fortune* magazine in 2003, 2004, and 2005. Darden Restaurants, the world's largest casual dining restaurant company, gave us their Distinguished Supplier Award in 2005, and Wendy's named us their Quality Supplier of the Year in 2003. These are just a few of many awards we've received over the years.

I'm proud of these affirmations of our corporation.

KNOW WHEN TO CHANGE, AND WHEN TO HOLD STEADY

People sometimes ask me for advice about how to make decisions concerning whether to hold steady in the direction they are growing or to make changes. I ask two sets of questions:

1. *Are you having a positive impact?* Are you seeing results? Are you seeing signs of growth and productivity?

2. *Are you bearing good fruit?* In other words, is your product good? Are your company values good? Are you doing good work? Are you giving the world a product that is truly beneficial or helpful? Are you helping change the marketplace or the world for the better? Is your reputation associated with excellence and integrity?

If both answers are yes, then keep doing what you're doing. Stick with what is working, and do more of it.

If an area of your business isn't showing signs of growth and productivity after your best efforts, prune it away.

If there's an area of your business that doesn't reflect excellence—a deficiency in your product or processes or reputation—fix it.

When it comes to retirement, I don't believe in it.

I have no intention of retiring. I get up every morning about five o'clock and try to get out of bed just before the alarm rings so I can turn it off before it disturbs Patty's sleep. I have coffee and take a quick look at the morning news. Then I fix my own breakfast of two eggs, one portion of turkey sausage, a piece of bread, and orange juice to drink. And then the day unfolds in any one of a thousand ways. I never know fully what any day will hold, but I'm always eager to find out what God has on my schedule and agenda.

★   ★   ★

As each one has received a gift, minister it to one another,
as good stewards of the manifold grace of God.
(1 Peter 4:10 NKJV)

15

SEE YOUR COMPANY AS GOD'S GIFT TO YOU

The older I get and the more experiences I have, the more thankful I am for every good thing in my life, every friend and loved one, and every experience I have had, those that seemed good at the time and those that seemed bad. I have an increasing awareness that all good things come from God, and that nothing we ever accomplish in this life is something we accomplish. Rather, God enables us to accomplish everything—ultimately for His purposes and His glory.

We have called our company Pilgrim's *Pride* to indicate that we are pleased with the high quality of our products and proud to be of service to others. In the end, our goal is for God to look upon us with pride—and see us as people who have reflected His Son to the world in a way that is pure, consistent, faithful, and effective.

TREMENDOUS GIFTS

There are several things that I believe most of us take for granted—things for which we should be very grateful every day. We have been given tremendous gifts. We need to see them as such and remember to say "thank You" to the Creator who gave them to us. There are at least seven distinctive categories of gifts upon which I place very high importance:

1. GIFTS OF LABOR

It is a privilege to be able to contribute something to the world at large—to use our time, talent, and energy to labor on behalf of others.

The tasks of our work are not all that important. The people for whom and with whom we work are important beyond calculation. We are especially blessed if we have work to do that we love.

Every conscious person who has some mental faculty remaining is capable of doing *some* form of work—setting goals, accomplishing tasks, and exercising his or her talents and abilities to produce something that has the potential to help others.

Our work may be physical or mental or both. It may be as employment or on a volunteer basis. It may be in the home for the family, in the community, at a place of business, or in elected or military service.

In the end, our goal is for God to look upon us with pride—and see us as people who have reflected His Son to the world in a way that is pure, consistent, faithful, and effective.

With the gifts associated with work and labor inevitably comes the gift of facing a challenge and conquering it. We can improve. We can overcome. We can make changes in our world. We do this through our work— by taking on a problem and putting our shoulders to the grindstone, literally or figuratively, to turn that problem into something that takes on the nature of a blessing.

As far as I'm concerned, there is no reason for a person *not* to work— and work as diligently, consistently, and as hard as possible. We were made to produce. From the opening chapters of the Bible, I see that we were given a command to "be fruitful and multiply; fill the earth and subdue it; have dominion over the fish of the sea, over the birds of the air, and over every living thing that moves on the earth" (Gen. 1:28 NKJV). That's work!

I believe we need to encourage people to work and, in some cases, to require that people work. Work is to the benefit of the worker—psychologically and materially. Every person needs to be rewarded according to the work he or she does, not only in terms of money and material benefits, but in terms of appreciation, recognition, and applause.

2. GIFTS OF INTERNAL AND EXTERNAL RESOURCES

Every person has inner and outer resources—in some measure. Each of us has been given a measure of faith. Each of us has certain inborn gifts, talents, and abilities. Each person has some control over an amount of material goods, including money. We may not have much—or we may have a great deal—in any of these categories. Whatever we have, we are called to be good stewards of it and to use it wisely to provide for our families and our personal needs, and to help provide for those around us who may have fallen on hard times.

3. GIFTS OF THE MIND AND HEART

We have some capacity to learn, to remember, and to give voice to ideas and opinions. We have the ability to make suggestions and to express appreciation and gratitude.

We have a tremendous privilege in our world today to be able to read and to exchange ideas freely—not only in books and literature, but in many interactive forms of media. We have the privilege of learning as much as we want to learn, about as many topics as we want to explore. No other generation has had such a privilege.

No matter how smart you are or how much you know, you can still know more. There is always something beneficial and uplifting to learn.

In addition to the ability to learn, we have the ability to express what we have learned—to reason our way to logical conclusions, to come up with workable solutions, to ask questions that prompt research and study, to overcome difficult problems, and to make wise decisions.

What is true for the mind is also true for the heart. We have the capacity to feel and to empathize with others. We have the ability to express sympathy and compassion. We have the ability to laugh, share joy, and provide tender encouragement to people who may be hurting.

Countless lonely and suffering people in the world long to receive a caring touch. We have some degree of ability to reach out and help these people. It is the ultimate gift of the heart—the expression of love—that makes life worth living.

4. GIFTS OF FAMILY AND FRIENDSHIP TIES

Each one of us has family, even if we never met our "blood" family and even if our family members have preceded us in death. We have a family heritage and bloodline into which we have been born.

Many of us have families of our own—a spouse and children, nephews, nieces, grandchildren, and even godchildren.

Each one of us has associates with the potential to become friends.

Time and again people are interviewed after great natural tragedies, having lost everything of material substance, and they will say as they cling to other members of their family, "We lost everything, but thank God, we have each other. We are alive and we are together."

The presence of other human beings in our lives—people to whom we can give love and from whom we can receive love—is a gift beyond measure.

5. GIFTS OF DREAMS AND ASPIRATIONS

We have the ability to envision something more that we might like to do, be, own, accomplish, or establish on the earth before we die. We have the ability to see ourselves as becoming better than we are, and as achieving more than we have. We have the ability to set goals and to make plans to meet these goals. What a tremendous gift this is to us! We are not robots. We can wish upon our own star and chart our own course toward the fulfillment of our dreams.

This gift to us of being able to see what currently isn't visible is called "faith" in the Bible—it is the ability to see God working on our behalf and for our benefit. (See Rom. 8:28 and Heb. 11:1.) We can use our gift of faith to trust in God and to believe for God's best and highest in those we love.

To a great extent, as we activate this gift of being able to dream and to aspire to greater things, we become motivated to use our gifts of labor and resources to maximum advantage. The gift of dreams and aspirations is very close to having hope and a strong sense of purpose for our lives.

6. GIFTS OF FREEDOM

We in the United States of America are blessed with tremendous gifts of freedom. We are free to voice our opinions, to meet together with other people in free assembly, to read a free press, and to vote for elected officials to whom we may freely express our likes and dislikes about the way our nation's business is conducted. We are free to pursue the religion of our choice. We are free to live where we want to live.

In America, we have the ability to pursue a destiny of our choice, at least to some degree, with a great deal of freedom. We can choose to read and study what we want to read and study, and to pursue challenges that we set for ourselves. We can aspire to new positions and roles. We can pursue new careers.

To be free does not mean, of course, that we can do anything we want to do. Your freedoms end at my nose, and vice versa. But we are free to pursue life, liberty, and the pursuit of happiness. We can choose to love and marry and have children. We can choose to start a business. We can choose which clubs and associations are worthy of our membership. We can choose our place of employment.

7. THE GIFT OF TODAY

We have the present. We don't know how many days are in our personal future. But we do have this moment, this hour, this day. We can make today count in any one of a thousand ways. What a gift to have one more day to do what we believe we have been put on this earth to do!

We have this day to work, and to use our internal and external resources to make a difference in this world.

We have this day to appreciate and associate with family members and friends; to express our love, gratitude, and praise; and to offer our best ideas and most creative suggestions for the benefit of others.

We have this day to pursue our dreams and hopes. We have this day to exercise our faith and to trust God for His highest and best in our lives.

We have this day to express our talents, give voice to our beliefs, and to give smiles and warm handshakes and hugs to those we encounter.

THESE CONCEPTS WORK IN THE WORKPLACE

"But," you may be saying, "what does any of this have to do with the creation of a corporate environment?"

It has everything to do with it. As an executive or leader in your place of business—and keep in mind that you can be a leader even though you don't have an official title of supervisor or manager—you have a tremendous opportunity to encourage and motivate others, and give them an opportunity to use the gifts they have been given. Let me offer you a few suggestions along these lines, running through the same categories I just used:

1. *Gift of labor.* You have the opportunity to encourage and to reward work in other people—to motivate them by your example, by your words of encouragement and advice, and by your directives—and to be diligent in producing work that is high in quality, efficient, and of good purpose. You have the opportunity to reward the efforts of others with a "thank you," a smile of encouragement, or a hand clasped on the shoulder as if to say, "Well done!" Recognize that work is a gift, and choose to activate that gift in yourself and others. When employees in any organization are

highly motivated to produce top-quality work, there's no end to the growth of that company or to the benefits that can come to individual employees.

2. *Gift of internal and external resources.* You have opportunities to use your distinctive talents, to express your optimism and hope, and to encourage others to do the same. Every person longs for *someone* who will see that he or she has potential and inspire him or her to develop it. You also have the opportunity from time to time to show up at the hospital bedside or at the funeral home, to give a gift that will help a person in a time of need, or to volunteer your services to those less fortunate. The more you give of your internal and external resources, the more others will be inspired to follow your example.

The more people develop their individual skills and abilities to the highest levels, the more a company can accomplish, the better customer service the company can provide, and the more the company can move toward setting the standards for its industry.

3. *Gift of mind and heart.* You have the opportunity to give information and to help others learn new things. You have the opportunity to solicit ideas and creative solutions from those with whom you work. You have the opportunity to challenge them to come up with innovative approaches, to resolve problems, and to offer suggestions that can help you and others make better decisions. You have the opportunity to encourage others to study and to use all of their mental abilities.

You also have the ability to express your concern for them—to model before them a person who genuinely cares, who is respectful, and who upholds the dignity of every person regardless of race or background. Be quick to give a smile and quick to laugh or express joy in appreciation of good news. If you work in an office setting, keep your door and your heart open to others around you. An open, joyful, and giving environment is a thoroughly enjoyable environment in which to work as well as to live.

4. *Gift of family and friends.* Every person comes to work every day from some type of family environment—or lack of a family. Every person tends to make friendships at work—at least to some degree. Expect this. Show your appreciation for the relationships that those in your sphere of influence may have. Remember to acknowledge special events and milestones in the family lives of your coworkers. Encourage those under your leadership to treat others in the workplace as extended family members—to genuinely care for one another and to be loyal to one another. This is the very essence of morale in the workplace.

5. *Gift of dreams and aspirations.* Encourage others who look to you for leadership to dream bigger dreams and set higher goals, even as you set the tone by sharing bigger dreams and setting higher goals for yourself and for your team, at work and in the community. Spur one another on to greater heights. The company that still sees the potential for growth will pursue the options to grow.

6. *Gift of freedom.* As a leader in your workplace, you know that the efficiency and productivity of your operation depend upon some structure—start and stop times of shifts and breaks, rules set out in an employee handbook, rules related to security and safety, and so forth. But as much as is possible, seize the opportunity to encourage free expression of ideas. Create opportunities for people to voice their ideas to you—even ones that may seem "out of the box." Create opportunities to share information, not only about the tasks in your work, but about the company and its accomplishments, the leaders and their needs, and the upcoming challenges and the way in which you intend to approach them.

You also have the opportunity to suggest that some of the people with whom you work might pursue their own potential in new ways—through seeking additional training or more formal education, taking on a new challenge, or receiving a promotion or transfer to a new position.

An organization in which communication and ideas flow freely is a creative organization, one that is much quicker to adapt to changing trends and to seize new business opportunities. An organization in which people are encouraged to reach their highest potential will be much better positioned to reach its highest potential.

7. *Gift of today.* Even as you dream and set goals, stay focused on the tasks of today. Make the most of every hour. Don't delay in saying "thank you" to someone, writing a good report, sharing an inspired idea, or offering a workable suggestion. Take the initiative in leading others to give their maximum effort to the tasks of the day, and to do so in positive ways.

These gifts that may sound philosophical are actually extremely sound business principles for creating a highly positive work environment—one that is productive, high in morale, responsive to beneficial changes and innovations, forward thinking and forward moving, and diligent on task. It is a compelling environment—people don't want to miss a day of work or an opportunity to shine.

In the end, your company is a gift to you. I awaken every morning keenly aware that I am very blessed to have another day to be the leader of Pilgrim's Pride.

What is a gift to you, you can make a gift to the world. I also awaken every morning keenly aware that I have the ability to expand the influence of Pilgrim's Pride, to offer even more and better products to my customers, to serve our Partners in even greater and more caring ways, and to leave behind something that is truly noteworthy to the world.

Giving and receiving make the world go around.

They also make life worth living.

★　★　★

Every good gift and every perfect gift is from above,
and comes down from the Father of lights, with whom
there is no variation or shadow of turning.
(James 1:17 NKJV)

16

FINDING PERSONAL BALANCE
AND FULFILLMENT

A while back, my wife, Patty, and I went over to Pine, Texas, to show an old friend, Frank Glover, around the little town where I grew up. Pine is not quite as small a town as it was when I was growing up there in the 1930s . . . but almost. Frank and I had a good time reminiscing about our early days. He has been a friend for more than forty years.

On the way home, Frank said to me, "Bo, if our lives were put on tape and we could rewind the tape, where would you like to stop the tape or make changes?" I had to think about that for a few seconds, but then I said, "If I could start over and know what I know now, I think I would be a preacher."

Frank seemed surprised at my reply. He reflected for a few moments and then said, "I think you *have* been a minister for the Lord."

I thought in that moment, *I hope so. That's the most important thing to me.*

Now, I don't have any regrets that I'm not a preacher or that my life took a different direction. I know that I've done what God desired for me to do. What I meant in my reply to Frank was this: In my opinion, the work of a preacher is the greatest work on this earth.

I care about producing the best-quality chickens, turkeys, and eggs that our Partners and I can produce. I care that people have sufficient protein in their diet and that rural America remains a vibrant, economically viable place for people to live and work. I care that people eat chicken—and more specifically I want them to eat Pilgrim's Pride chicken!

But even more, I care about what happens to a person's soul.

The price of poultry rises and falls, sometimes daily but certainly in broader cycles. People eat, and then the next day, they eat again. The decisions related to a person's soul, however, are eternal. Preaching the gospel is work that has a divine dimension to it.

Can a businessman be a preacher? I like to think he can!

A RIGHT PRIORITY OF COMMITMENTS

My commitment to the Lord is the first priority in my life. It is followed by my family, then Pilgrim's Pride. If you have your priorities right, and your character is right, then the only thing remaining is to practice good management principles—and do so with honesty and integrity. You must have a high energy level and treat people right, and from my perspective, there's not much more that's required to succeed personally or in business.

As I indicated earlier, the year my father died was the year I accepted Jesus Christ as my personal Savior. The pastor made an appeal at the close of his sermon one Sunday, and I didn't respond immediately. Actually I had already made my way to the back of the church. There, at the entrance, I realized that if I wanted to spend eternity with my father, who was a godly man and a leader in that small Baptist church in Pine, I needed to get things right with God. I said to the friends with me, "I'm going forward. You're going forward, too." They walked the aisle with me.

I don't know how many of those boys actually meant what they confessed about Jesus Christ that day, but I know that I meant what I said from the bottom of my heart. I knew I had made things right with God, and I was forgiven of my sins. From that day on, I had a life of greater purpose, fulfillment, and witness ahead of me. It was a critical juncture in my life. It was a decision I've never regretted making for even one second.

Very soon after I made that decision, I made a second decision. I needed to be involved in a church, not just attend one. I needed to give back to the Lord, not only of my money and of my presence, but of my time and talent. I am still living out those decisions.

On Sunday mornings you can find me in the former boardroom of Pilgrim Bank. Now you might think that's an odd place for me to be since I am very open about my Christian faith, my belief in the Bible, and my concern that people keep the Ten Commandments, one of which commands us to keep the Sabbath day holy.

Let me quickly add that you will find me in the bank boardroom on Sunday mornings because that's where my Sunday School class meets!

Several years ago the class asked if there was a more comfortable place they could meet—by comfortable they meant a place with comfortable chairs, a table on which to put their Bibles and take notes, and enough room to spread out a little. The class suggested that we meet at the bank, which is just across the street from the church. I was glad to oblige. Not only was it Pilgrim Bank, but I'm the teacher of the class.

I've been teaching Sunday School for more than fifty years now.

I teach every Sunday I'm in Pittsburg—and since I make it a point to be in Pittsburg on Sundays, that's almost every Sunday.

MY FAMILY CAN'T BE REPLACED

Patty and I have two sons and a daughter, and six grandchildren. They are tremendous blessings to me.

Like most fathers, I'm very proud of my children. My two sons, Ken and Pat, are involved in the company. Both sons are in positions that are geared to their temperaments and talents. I'm proud of the work they do.

My beautiful daughter, Greta, lives in Dallas with her family. She's a joy to be around, and there are many days when I wish she also lived in Pittsburg so we could see more of her and her children. Greta is also involved in the company.

I first met my wife, Patty, at her cousin's wedding. She was a brides-maid, and I was her escorting usher. It didn't take me long to conclude that the *next* wedding I wanted to see her at was ours—with her as the bride and me as the groom. Patty is ten years younger than I am so when I first went to call on Patty and meet her parents, they weren't particularly thrilled to see me show up. Patty was just a teenager and there I was, an "old man" in my late twenties in a struggling business. Nevertheless, I think they saw that I had some potential to give Patty a good life, and they certainly must have seen that I was head over heels crazy about their daughter. Who wouldn't have been? Patty was and is one of the most beautiful women I've ever known. She is also one of the sweetest and kindest women on this earth.

I'm glad for her sweetness and kindness because when it comes to life at home, she's my boss.

Not long ago I was talking to a woman who helps us at the house, and I mentioned to her that Patty and I have been together for forty-nine years now. She asked if I had any secrets for such a long and good mar-riage, and I said, "Well, when we disagree, I say my piece and she says her piece and then she says, 'And you know where the front door is' . . . and I give in."

The housekeeper and I shared a good laugh about that, but there's a great truth in that little exchange, and it doesn't have anything to do with who gets his or her way in a marriage. In any relationship—at work, at home, in the community—there's something more important than win-ning an argument. It's remaining in a relationship.

Patty is also the one who keeps me grounded. With all the talk of pride associated with the name Pilgrim, it's good to have somebody to keep you humble!

I've had a lot of attention in my life—a lot of high-profile attention. My silhouette profile cameo is on lots of things—every truck in our fleet, our office buildings, mills, and plants. The silhouette profile is also on the bank's new credit and debit cards. And I've already mentioned the big likeness of my head and shoulders outside the distribution center in Pittsburg.

My wife, Patty, isn't much on that high-profile stuff. She keeps my feet on the ground.

I enjoy meeting people so I enjoy the parties at the governor's mansion or the dinners with various people who are considered famous. I see them as people, and I like meeting people. After all, every one of them is a potential chicken consumer. But when it comes to a high profile, the only real reason for me to have one personally is to promote Pilgrim's Pride. It's a matter of advertising.

There are lots of places I don't need to be in the foreground, and I'm not. When I'm at church on Sunday, I'm in the background. That's not the place for advertising or being onstage. That's the time for sitting in a pew with Patty by my side.

At work I need to be in charge. In the commercials and promotional opportunities I need to strut and crow. Once I take off my Pilgrim duds and set Henrietta down, I am content to sit quietly among the flock.

A PERSONAL JOB DESCRIPTION

ROOTED IN SERVICE TO GOD

Like all corporations, Pilgrim's Pride Corporation has job descriptions and job titles. My official title is cofounder and chairman.

Beyond my corporate job description, however, I have a personal job description that isn't linked to Pilgrim's Pride. It's linked to the way I see myself in relationship to my ultimate boss, Jesus Christ.

A number of years ago I was challenged to write a personal job description for the way I saw my role and purpose as God's servant on the earth. I review this and update it periodically. I have found it extremely beneficial to me to do this and also to list specific activities (daily, weekly, monthly) and key areas related to the job description.

Here's the job description I've tried to fulfill for some time now. I update it and sign it again at the beginning of each year:

Title: Servant—Bo Pilgrim

Date written: January 5, 2005

Reports to: God through Jesus Christ

Purpose: Serving God through worship, fellowship, discipleship, ministry, and missions/evangelism in His church as directed by His purpose, which was planned before I was born.

I'm a member of the First Baptist Church of Pittsburg, Texas. I consider it my greatest honor to be a trustee of the Lord. The Lord owns everything on this earth. When I give, I am only giving what belongs to Him already.

Activities: Under this heading, I listed sixteen things that relate to my personal devotional life and work in my local church—things such as attending church regularly, reading my Bible daily, and being in a state of readiness (awareness) to meet Jesus any moment.

Key impact areas: I listed these five areas that I believe to be directly related to a person with my job description: worship (exalting Jesus Christ), fellowship with the church as the family of God, discipleship (teaching others to glorify God in all things), ministry of service to others, and missions/evangelism to help people find salvation in Jesus Christ.

In many companies, key impact areas are analyzed according to the percentage of a person's time and the percentage of importance. Here's how I broke down these impact areas:

	% Distribution of Importance	% Distribution of Time
Worship	20%	24%
Fellowship	15%	22%
Discipleship	25%	20%
Ministry	15%	14%
Missions/Evangelism	25%	20%

In addition, I wrote down a number of statements in each of these areas that are good reminders to me of the perspective and character traits I want to embody, and the things I want to do to engage in these activities.

Key impact standards: I wrote out specific ways of measuring my success at actually doing my job in the five areas I identified. For example, under "Missions/Evangelism" I put "Number of Good News booklets I give away each week."

Strategy: Finally I wrote out a statement of overall strategy for implementing this job description, taking into consideration the key impact areas and all that I had written related to them and to the standards for measuring my progress. This strategy statement had fewer than thirty words.

This is one of the most beneficial exercises I've ever done personally. I highly recommend the process to you. It can really help you clarify your purpose on this earth, not just your job description in a company.

Who we are as people—now and forever—is of utmost importance. The things we accomplish help make us who we are, but more important, who we are in the broader scope of time and eternity greatly affects the things we accomplish.

GIVING AWAY
MY LITTLE BLACK BOOK

You may have noted that when it comes to the way I see my work in missions and evangelism, I listed, "Number of Good News booklets I give away each week." Actually I call this booklet my "little black book."

My heart surgery and heart attack more than twenty years ago spurred me to something on a more personal level to share my faith with other people. I spent some time considering just what it is that I would want to say to a person about how to become a Christian. I read through the major booklets of organizations such as Campus Crusade for Christ ("The Four Spiritual Laws"), and I read different versions of the Bible. This little booklet is the result of what I selected to be the most concise and effective way in which I personally would like to share the gospel with another person.

The booklet has twelve pages that are graduated in size for easy reference, and it is only 3 by 4½ inches in overall size—just the right size to slip into a shirt pocket. If we were talking face-to-face right now, I'd hand you one of these booklets to have as your own, but since that's not possible, let me share with you the entire contents:

STEP 1: *There is a reason you need to be saved: Sin!*
(All Scripture below is from THE LIVING BIBLE.)

- Yes, all have sinned; all fall short of God's glorious ideal.—Rom. 3:23

- As the Scriptures say, "No one is good—no one in all the world is innocent." No one has ever really followed God's paths, or even truly wanted to. Everyone has turned away; all have gone wrong. No one anywhere has kept on doing what is right; not one.
  —Rom. 3:10–12

- That man is a fool who says to himself, "There is no God!" Anyone who talks like that is warped and evil and cannot really be a good person at all. The Lord looks down from heaven on all mankind to see if there are any who are wise, who want to please God. But no, all have strayed away; all are rotten with sin. Not one is good, not one!—Ps. 14:1–3

- The heart is the most deceitful thing there is, and desperately wicked. No one can really know how bad it is!—Jer. 17:9

STEP 2: *There is a penalty for your sin—*
Death! Eternal Death!

- For the wages of sin is death, but the free gift of God is eternal life through Jesus Christ our Lord.—Rom. 6:23

- And just as it is destined that men die only once, and after that comes judgment.—Heb. 9:27

- You may eat any fruit in the garden except fruit from the Tree of Conscience—for its fruit will open your eyes to make you aware of right and wrong, good and bad. If you eat its fruit, you will be doomed to die.—Gen. 2:17

- When Adam sinned, sin entered the entire human race. His sin spread death throughout all the world, so everything began to grow old and die, for all sinned.—Rom. 5:12

- These evil thoughts lead to evil actions and afterward to the death penalty from God.—James 1:15

STEP 3: *God has made the provision*
for your condition—Christ!

- When we were utterly helpless with no way of escape, Christ came at just the right time and died for us sinners who had no use for him. But God showed His great love for us by sending Christ to die for us while we were still sinners. And since by His blood He did all this for us as sinners, how much more will He do for us now that He has declared us not guilty? Now He will save us from all of God's wrath to come.—Rom. 5:6, 8–9

- God paid a ransom to save you from the impossible road to heaven which your fathers tried to take, and the ransom He paid was not mere gold or silver, as you very well know. But He paid for you with the precious lifeblood of Christ, the sinless, spotless Lamb of God.—1 Pet. 1:18–19

- He is the one who took God's wrath against our sins upon himself, and brought us into fellowship with God; and He is the forgiveness for our sins and not only ours but all the world's. —1 John 2:2

- For God loved the world so much that He gave His only Son so that anyone who believes in Him shall not perish but have eternal life.—John 3:16

- I passed on to you right from the first what had been told to me, that Christ died for our sins just as the Scriptures said He would, and that He was buried, and that three days afterward He arose from the grave just as the prophets foretold.—1 Cor. 15:3–4

STEP 4: *Your response to*
God's provision—Believe!

- For if you tell others with your own mouth that Jesus Christ is your Lord, and believe in your own heart that God has raised Him from the dead, you will be saved. For it is by believing in his heart that a man becomes right with God; and with his mouth he tells others of his faith, confirming his salvation. Anyone who calls upon the name of the Lord will be saved.—Rom. 10:9–10, 13

- But to all who received Him, He gave the right to become children of God. All they needed to do was to trust Him to save them.—John 1:12

- Look! I have been standing at the door and I am constantly knocking. If anyone hears Me calling him and opens the door I will come in and fellowship with him and he with Me.—Rev. 3:20

- I have written this to you who believe in the Son of God so that you may know you have eternal life.—1 John 5:13

- There is no eternal doom awaiting those who trust Him to save them. But those who don't trust Him have already been tried and condemned for not believing in the only Son of God.—John 3:18

INVITATION

(All Scripture below is from the NEW KING JAMES VERSION.)

Will you now receive CHRIST as your personal SAVIOR? You know you are a sinner . . . you know CHRIST died for you, for YOUR SINS.

> *Will you, by faith, pray this prayer:*
> *"Lord Jesus, be merciful to me a sinner. Save me now . . .*
> *I give You my life now and forever. Amen!"*

After these four steps I put a page of what I call the "ordinances"—the things we must do as Christians, whether we have just received Christ or have been serving Him for many years:

OBEDIENCE

Follow Christ in Baptism:
"And he commanded them to be baptized in the name of the Lord."—Acts 10:48

Study Your Bible:
"Search the scriptures . . ."—John 5:39

"As newborn babes, desire the sincere milk of the word, that ye may grow thereby."—1 Pet. 2:2

"And now, brethren, I commend you to God, and to the word of His grace, which is able to build you up."—Acts 20:32

Pray Daily:

"Be careful for nothing; but in every thing by prayer and supplication with thanksgiving let your request be made known unto God."—Phil. 4:6

"And He spake a parable unto them to this end, that men ought always to pray, and not to faint."—Luke 18:1

Attend Church Regularly:

"Not forsaking the assembling of ourselves together, as the manner of some is."—Heb. 10:25

Witness to Others:

"He that winneth souls is wise."—Prov. 11:30

And finally I added the Ten Commandments since so many people these days don't seem to know what they are, and in some areas, these commandments are being removed from public buildings. (All of the Scripture below is from the NEW INTERNATIONAL VERSION.)

JESUS AND THE TEN COMMANDMENTS
The Ten Commandments say . . .

Exodus 20:3
"You shall have no other gods before me."

Exodus 20:4
"You shall not make for yourself an idol."

Exodus 20:7
"You shall not misuse the name of the LORD your God."

Exodus 20:8
"Remember the Sabbath day by keeping it holy."

Exodus 20:12
"Honor your father and your mother."

Exodus 20:13
"You shall not murder."

Exodus 20:14
"You shall not commit adultery."

Exodus 20:15
"You shall not steal."

Exodus 20:16
"You shall not give false testimony."

Exodus 20:17
"You shall not covet."

I tuck a folded $20 bill into the back of the booklets that I carry in my pocket, and I'm quick to give away these booklets to people I meet. I usually ask, "Have you ever seen my little black book?" If they have, I don't try to give one. But if they haven't, I ask, "Would you like a copy?"

Most people are curious—a few may even think I'm talking about a book of names and phone numbers—and they will accept the booklet from me. For those who discover the $20 bill in the back—well, the reaction is very predictable. A big smile will come on their faces, and they usually say something to the effect, "Did you mean for this to be there?" Absolutely.

A few years ago I was in the lobby of a large hotel, and I looked across the room and saw Ted Turner, the founder of CNN, sitting by himself. I went over to him and introduced myself. I knew he owned a large cattle ranch so I figured we at least had agriculture in common. I'm not sure he had ever met a chicken farmer from Texas, and he seemed moderately interested. I gave him a copy of my little black book, and he thumbed through it quickly. When he saw the $20 bill, he took it out and said, "I don't need your money."

I replied, "I'm sure you don't, but it comes with the booklet. The $20 bill is a sign that I'm serious about what I'm saying. I want the people who receive this booklet to know that I'm also very serious about their taking the time to read it, so serious that I'll even give them something for their time." Ted Turner smiled and tucked the $20 back into the booklet, and we went our separate ways. I don't know if he read the booklet—I hope so.

Not long ago I received an invitation to speak to a group of pastors, missionaries, and young people—about three thousand were expected to attend the event. I agreed to go, and very quickly I did the math. I felt an urgency to let the bank know that I would be needing $60,000 worth of $20 bills so I could give each person in attendance one of my little black books.

The bank wasn't all that surprised at my request. Neither was the printer who got the rush order to print three thousand copies.

I'm glad they weren't surprised.

The people who received the booklets *were* surprised . . . and grateful.

I'm glad they were. I know they'll be *eternally* grateful if they heed what the booklet says!

★   ★   ★

For what will it profit a man if he gains the whole
world, and loses his own soul?
(Mark 8:36 NKJV)

17

LIFE AT THE CHATEAU

Patty and I live in Chateau de Pilgrim. It's a large home in the French Baroque classical style of architecture—more specifically it is in the style of Louis XV. If you are driving along Highway 271 south of Pittsburg, you can't miss it.

Some of the local citizens of Pittsburg refer to the house as Cluckingham Palace. It's something of a visible landmark in the Pittsburg area—and yes, it is fairly palatial. We knew it would be so we put the Pilgrim-hat profile of my likeness in the wrought-iron gates at the front entrance. At least we get some advertising benefit for those who are driving in front of our home!

Now Patty and I aren't French, we don't consider ourselves nobility, and there are just the two of us at home these days. So why build a house of this size, style, and grandeur on the outskirts of Pittsburg, Texas?

There were several reasons.

A REFLECTION OF WHAT WE LIKE

The house is a reflection of things we like and value. Even though the house may look very elegant from the outside, the Louis XV period of style was noted for very well-mannered dignity, symmetry, and functional practicality. I like these features. They appeal to my sense of order and my engineering tendencies to blend together function and form. The house has a great deal of light, and it tolerates a mix of different interior styles. Patty especially likes these features since she is an artist.

A Place for Our Collections

Patty and I developed an appreciation for French art and antiques through the years. We have a fairly extensive collection of French classical antiques. However, not all of the rooms are furnished with French furniture. Some are English, including one bedroom done in Victorian style. Patty has her collection of dolls there. She enjoys doll making and china painting.

The pool house, the exercise room, and the media room are American!

A Showcase of Creation

Houses of this type were known in Europe for their gardens. Well, gardening to me is a form of farming. I believe the twenty-five-acre grounds on which the house is situated present a wonderful opportunity to showcase the beauty of God's creative nature.

One of the ways I relax is by driving a big tractor pulling a bush hog behind it. There's something rewarding about clearing the land and tilling it up. I did a significant amount of the land clearing for the grounds of Chateau de Pilgrim. The landscape architect once told me that he was surprised at how quickly I cleared the land as he had requested. He said he knew from that moment that he'd have to march double-time to stay ahead of me on the design of the acreage.

We have placed a number of sculptures in the formal gardens to the front, side, and back of the house. Some of them are of our grandchildren—and some are of chickens and baby chicks. Some sculptures are of deer and swans. There's a sculpture of me sitting by the lily pond on a rustic log bench. I have an open Bible on my knees. There's enough room on the bench for a person to sit down. I insisted that the writing on the Bible be clear enough to read—it's one of my favorite passages. It is Luke 9:23–26:

> And He said to them all, "If any *man* will come after me, let him deny himself, and take up his cross daily, and follow me. For whosoever would save his life shall lose it; but whosoever will lose his life for my sake, the same shall save it. For what is a man profited, if he gains the whole world, and lose himself, or be cast away? For whosoever shall be ashamed of me and of my words, of him shall the Son of man be ashamed, when he shall come in his own glory, and in his father's, and of the holy angels." (New Scofield Ref. Ed. Oxford, Authorized KING JAMES VERSION)

We also have large informal gardens with a small lake, a turtle pond, an azalea forest, a real bog, and an area for wildflowers. Across the fence is acreage we own that we've left in its pristine meadow state.

We used a wide variety of plants, most of which are labeled at their base using the same labeling system as the Dallas Arboretum. We have worked with our landscape architect to plant some experimental plants, such as varieties of azaleas, that have not been released to the public, as well as rare and unusual plants not typically seen in East Texas. These planted areas remind us of God's infinite variety and beauty in creation. We have more than two miles of asphalted roads and walking paths that go throughout the property—these are great for exercise as well as walks intended purely for personal reflection and prayer.

The gardens have sitting areas, fountains, and plenty of color. In the spring, we are treated to the glory of more than 150 varieties and species of bulbs.

Across the back fence is open pasture for horses, and in the distance, you can see several chicken houses.

Patty and I fully expect that one day the house may become something of a museum and botanical center.

A Place to Host and Entertain

The Chateau has given us many wonderful opportunities for entertaining our friends. We have also had opportunities to sponsor fund-raising events, and to give hospitable, quiet, and secure shelter to guests from the political, business, and entertainment worlds. When George W. Bush was running for governor of Texas, we were privileged to host a barbecue for about a thousand of his supporters on the back lawn, and were also privileged to have George, Laura, and their daughters as our houseguests. George and the girls really seemed to enjoy the pool.

A Place to
Inspire Dreams in Others

Chateau de Pilgrim doesn't look anything at all like what a boy from Pine, Texas, might one day have as a home. That may be the foremost reason for building this house—it's a testament to our human ability to dream big dreams and trust God to fulfill them as He sees fit.

As a boy, I never saw a house like the Chateau. I didn't know they existed! And when I finally learned that such houses did exist, they were off in Europe or other faraway places, built for another era and social status.

The Chateau de Pilgrim sends a message that people in *rural* America can build great companies, make good money, buy things and enjoy things they like—even a French-style chateau in the midst of East Texas. They can leave behind something of beauty and elegance for future generations. Grandeur and luxury are not only possible, but enjoyable—as long as items of grandeur and luxury don't become idols or a person's sole preoccupation.

A house like the Chateau de Pilgrim—which is unlike any other house I know, and certainly unlike any other house in my town of Pittsburg—also sends a message of personal creativity and individuality. I'm not like anybody else, never have been, won't ever be, and don't want to be. The same is true for you. Each of us is a one-of-a-kind design, handcrafted by the Creator of the universe. He never does anything exactly the same way, and He delights in making each one of us unique. Our house reflects that aspect of God's creation.

I don't encourage the young people to whom I speak from time to time to dream about houses that are like other people's houses or like my house, any more than I encourage young people to try to become just like someone else in their expression of their talents. We are called to be distinctively original—totally ourselves—and yet reflect the character absolutes that are most godly. What a privilege that is!

I live in my house. My closest friends feel comfortable coming over to visit me at my house. Patty's friends feel the same way. I especially enjoy working at home in the pool house because it has such great amounts of light and such a fantastic view out over the back gardens and fields. I don't feel the least bit embarrassed or defensive about having a beautiful place in which to live, entertain, pray, conduct business, or socialize with friends. The house is a blessing, and I thank God for it.

> *Each of us is a one-of-a-kind design, handcrafted by the Creator of the universe. He never does anything exactly the same way, and He delights in making each one of us unique. Our house reflects that aspect of God's creation.*

Would I build this house again just as we built it? Definitely. I made only two mistakes in building Chateau de Pilgrim. The first mistake was that I told the architects to be creative. The second mistake was that I didn't have a budget. If I were building the house again, I might put just a few more limits on the creativity and the budget. And then again, I might not. The Chateau will certainly be a landmark long after Patty and I are in heaven.

What about you?

I don't know how you live or where you live, but I encourage you in these areas:

- Create a place in which you feel totally comfortable with yourself, your family, your friends.
- Create a place that is a tribute to God—a place of beauty, harmony, and peace. Create a place where you have no hesitancy to pray or to talk to others about the Lord.
- Create a place that is a reflection of things you like, appreciate, and enjoy. Don't copy somebody else's style just for the sake of being stylish according to general norms.
- Create a place that works for you—that allows you to function to the maximum of your abilities, including your maximum ability to dream and plan and envision new horizons.
- Create a place that causes others to reflect upon God's goodness and God's great diversity of creation.

Do the same when it comes to the office in which you work. And if you have a second office in which you meet people or a conference room in which you meet with groups of people, extend these principles to those environments.

Create an environment in which you are comfortable and others are comfortable—a place that is peaceful and pleasant, a place that is functional and yet comfortable, a place that reflects your personality, and a place that is distinctively *you*.

What does all this have to do with business?

When you create an environment that is uniquely your own, you send a signal that you are comfortable in your own skin and that you have a strong sense of purpose and direction for your life. That sends a signal to others—even if they don't particularly like your style—that you likely have the same sense of purpose, direction, and distinctiveness for your company. If you have a clear vision for your life, in all likelihood, you have a clear vision for your company.

A strong, clear vision usually results in a strong, bright future.

★　★　★

Now therefore, let it please You to bless the house of
Your servant, that it may continue before You forever.
(2 Sam. 7:29 NKJV)

18

THE BOTTOM LINE:
KNOW WHO TO CREDIT

Every businessperson is concerned with the bottom line. Even more important, in my opinion, is the bottom line for life.

I am hopeful that my company will continue to be one of the leaders in the poultry industry—not only in volume and financial figures, but in quality and value. We have had wonderful success stories through the years made possible by the dedication and hard work of thousands of people—not just me. I believe our leadership is poised for a very positive future. The corporation operates with outstanding people in a strong and growing industry. There is every reason to believe we will have an excellent future.

But I also know with absolute certainty that Pilgrim's Pride will continue to succeed only as long as those connected to it understand the *real*

Just recently I was given a financial statement by my accountant. It indicated that I have achieved a milestone: I have a combined net worth of $1 billion. Not one cent of it belongs to me. It all belongs to the Lord.

reason for the company's existence and the *real* reason for their personal existence on this earth, and that is to give God the credit and to give God the glory for everything good that is accomplished. If the leaders will continue to trust God and give Him the credit for their success, I have no hesitation in predicting that the 75th anniversary of Pilgrim's Pride in 2021 will truly be a mind-boggling thing!

In the end, the amount of money a person has isn't what really counts. It's what a person does with that money. It doesn't matter if a person has a little or a lot—it's all God's money anyway.

Just recently I was given a financial statement by my accountant. It indicated that I have achieved a milestone: I have a combined net worth of $1 billion.

Not one cent of it belongs to me. It all belongs to the Lord.

Two of the most important Scripture verses to me are these:

> Do not boast about tomorrow,
> For you do not know what a day may bring forth.
> Let another man praise you,
>   and not your own mouth;
> A stranger, and not your own lips. (Prov. 27:1–2 NKJV)

> The world and all that is in it belong to the Lord;
> The earth and all who live on it are His. (Ps. 24:1 TEV)

That's the bottom line.

About the Author

With his buckled Pilgrim hat, Bo Pilgrim has been a bona fide celebrity in the poultry business for many years. But he is also known as a deeply religious man with impeccable character, family-based values, and a warm, generous spirit. In turning a small farm supply store into a multi-billion-dollar company, Mr. Pilgrim has also kept honesty and integrity at the forefront and his priorities in simple perspective. His company is a successful, growing business made up of people who enjoy their work and produce good results for the company's stakeholders.

Some of the more recent accolades Pilgrim's Pride has received include:

- 2003: Wendy's Quality Supplier of the Year
- 2004: *Provisioner* magazine's "Cool Dozen Award," recognition of Pilgrim's Pride as one of the top twelve meat and poultry companies to work for
- 2005: Distinguished Supplier Award from Darden Restaurants, the world's largest casual dining restaurant company
- 2003, 2004, 2005: One of the "Most Admired Companies in America" named by *Fortune* magazine

Mr. Pilgrim has been a devoted husband to his wife, Patty, for 49 years. They have two sons, a daughter, and six grandchildren.

He teaches Sunday School almost every Sunday at the First Baptist Church in Pittsburg, Texas.

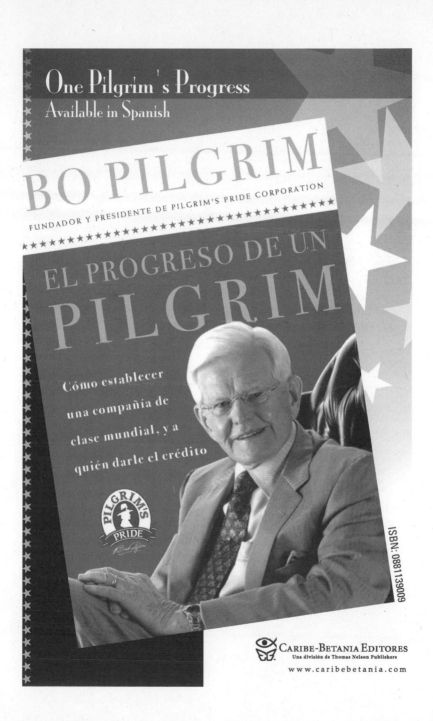